# a modern way to cook

# ANNA JONES

# a modern way to cook

**150+ vegetarian recipes
for quick, flavor-packed meals**

Ten Speed Press
Berkeley

For Laura.
How lucky I am to have been put here
with you as my sister.

And for my boy Dylan.
Your calming presence came before you.
I am blessed beyond measure to be your Mum.

I'll make you some promises about the food in this book:

- It's delicious, everyday food that will always be ready in a life-friendly amount of time.

- All the recipes are packed with tricks to help you be smarter in the kitchen.

- The recipes are full of fantastic ingredients that will leave you feeling great.

- You will make amazing vegetables the focus of your meals as you eat through the seasons.

- And my hope is that, over time, these recipes will make you more aware of what you put into your body in the same way they have for me.

Food for me is a celebration: three opportunities a day to sit, share, and revel in nourishing myself and others with amazing ingredients. Being in my kitchen allows me to connect with far-flung locations I have traveled; it firmly roots me in the time, place, and season, such as when I see the blood oranges arrive just after Christmas or the wild garlic herald the first days of spring. It's these things that inform my cooking, day in, day out.

But I'm just the same as the next person. For all of us, our lives are busier than they have ever been. We have access to so much, and the world is at our fingertips like never before. While this is brilliant in many ways, it also comes with the temptation to try and fit even more into already jam-packed lives.

I have been overwhelmed by the positive response to my first book, *A Modern Way to Eat*. The world of social media has allowed me to be directly in contact with the wonderful people who have been cooking from it, and I've noticed that the stuff they've been getting excited about hasn't been the fancy cakes or showy dinners but the easy weeknight recipes, which have been cooked again and again.

From what I have seen, there is a sense that people are more energized about cooking—we are reaping the benefits of home-cooked, vegetable-focused food. We have more connection to what we are eating, and our relationship to what we eat seems to be becoming more balanced. Also we feel genuinely happy and excited about the food we are putting on our tables. It's proof to me that food is a powerful force for change and that what we eat can completely transform our outlook on life. The e-mails I receive on a weekly basis are evidence that there is a huge wave of change happening, which is an incredible thing.

From my experience working in homes, schools, and kitchens, with kids, adults, parents, and lunch ladies, I know for a fact that sitting down to a nourishing home-cooked meal every day can have a massive impact on our minds, bodies, and overall happiness. It shouldn't just be something we do for a Sunday lunch or once in a blue moon. Cooking a homemade meal is the single most important thing we can do for our well-being, because then we know exactly what is going into our bodies. It allows us to honor the people we are cooking it for and it means that we also get a chance to sit round a table, eat, drink, and really spend time with one another.

The more I cook simply—easy pastas, quick hearty salads, and all-in-one gratins—the more I realize that food doesn't need to be posh, complicated, or made from exotic ingredients to do us good. It's the quick-to-make, everyday, and weeknight meals that we eat on, say, Tuesdays and Wednesdays that make a real difference in our lives. These meals are the "bread and butter" of our eating week and the most important ones to focus on.

At the same time that we are busier than ever, there is also a movement toward balancing things out. There's a desire to treat our bodies well and to look after ourselves physically, mentally, and spiritually. And an awful lot of this centers around the food we eat.

There has been a real shift in the way we look at food. More people are conscious of what they're putting into their shopping baskets, more people are buying seasonally, and more people are cooking at home. For the first time in two generations, home cooking is firmly back in fashion, and an ever-increasing number of people are actively choosing to eat a diet centered around vegetables on at least a few days of the week.

Making vegetables the focus of our diet is widely considered to be the single most important thing we can do for our own health and for the health of the planet. Over the last couple of years, eating a plant-based diet has moved from the domain of brightly painted vegetarian cafés to proud center stage.

I hope this book will show you how to do this in your home without too much fuss. It's packed full of the food I like to eat and the food I like to cook. To my mind, it's this straight-up everyday food that is so important for us to get right and get enthused about. And it's the recipes in this book that I hope will help you cook amazing, achievable meals every night of the week.

This book is my notebook of recipes, over 150 of them, flavor-packed with layers of texture and goodness. I hope they will revolutionize how you cook and eat in the same way they have in my home. It's modern cooking—making the most

of a rainbow of grains and vegetables and using flavor and texture to transform your dinners into quick and easy feasts.

They're recipes I am really proud of. From super-clever and ridiculously quick fifteen-minute one-pot pasta, to a Buddha bowl curry feast that would be grand enough to grace any table, this is the food that makes me happy. The sort that drives my cooking, led by flavor, texture, and a deep love and respect for food.

## Eating well

I am passionate about eating food that makes me feel good, and while I'll sometimes reach for a trashy chocolate bar or a heavy pub roast (which is all part of being human and nothing to be ashamed of), I know that's not the food that I feel good eating.

I want standout, delicious food that leaves me feeling energized, light, bright, and satisfied. It's this intersection between wellness and deliciousness that I strive for with every plate of food I make and eat. And with all the talk of health and wellness in the food industry, I think this sweet spot is becoming ever more important. Wellness doesn't come at the expense of deliciousness.

I welcome with open arms the new breadth of information and attention around eating well, and I am so thrilled that we are all putting more focus on what we put into our bodies and on the connection between the food we eat and how vibrantly we live.

But I also think it's important to remember that we are all individuals, each with our own completely separate nutritional needs. I can tell you what works for my body, but I honestly can't tell you exactly what's going to work for yours. Nor, in my opinion, can any chef or, really, any nutritionist. While nutritionists can absolutely be a guide, it is you who have to do the work. You need to have a relationship with your body and take responsibility for listening to it and how it reacts to certain foods. If you feel tired and bloated after eating something, make a change next time—eat a smaller portion, or try a different way of cooking or another ingredient.

There are lots of people out there ready to name superfoods that can help us lose weight, cure illness, and make us more attractive and amazing. It sometimes feels to me as though all this sometimes over-the-top focus on nutrition and "clean eating" has almost become the new, more acceptable way to be on a diet. And in a weird way, that isn't promoting a healthy attitude to food at all.

It's important to make a commitment to eating well, but it's also important to be realistic. Cooking goodness-packed meals every night is going to have a huge impact on your health, and simply getting more vegetables into your diet is a great first step. You can worry about matcha and chia seeds later on.

To me, eating well is far more simple than it is often made out to be. Buy good ingredients, cook at home, make the majority of what you eat plants and vegetables, and listen and react to your body. I don't think it's much more complicated than that. Right now, too many sweeping generalizations are being made in the world of food. Foods like bread are being vilified, and chefs and nutritionists are making blanket statements about how certain staple, cheap, and useful nutritious foods are unduly bad for our bodies. I think this is damaging, as it means our psychology around these foods changes. We attach guilt and a "forbidden" label to food, increasing our anxiety around it and causing us to crave it even more.

My point here is this: let's stop looking at food in its respective parts, and making some food bad and some disproportionately good. Let's get back to the whole picture, the whole food. Choosing a balanced way of eating, and sticking as close to nature as we possibly can, is the most realistic plan for eating long-term. Going to extremes is not a sustainable way of eating or living. What I am proposing here and with the recipes in this book is a sensible, flexible dietary strategy that we can incorporate into our lives successfully and joyfully, day-to-day and over a lifetime.

## The practice of quick, calm cooking

At home, I cook under the same constraints as anyone else. Even though I have a food background, when I come home from a day at work, feeling sometimes jaded with food, the last thing I want to do is spend hours at the stove. I am impatient and usually hungry, and I relish the art of cooking quickly. And that's what I want to share with you in this book. The clever secrets that chefs and cooks use, quick ways of cooking, smart cheats, and ways of working logically that have your dinner on the table in a friendly and achievable amount of time. All of this can happen in a calm and well-choreographed manner that won't leave your kitchen looking like a bomb site and use every pan in the cupboard.

These recipes are designed to come together relatively quickly. I asked a kind band of brilliant friends who aren't cooks to test and time themselves, and they proved my point.

The recipes that take 15 minutes are quick supper dishes, delicious and simple, with just a few ingredients that come together in one pan without much chopping or fuss. The recipes that are ready in 20 to 30 minutes are a little more advanced, with more complex layers of flavor and texture and a few more ingredients, while those that take 40 minutes are real feasts, riots of flavor and color that I would happily eat at any restaurant table.

In addition to these chapters, this book pivots around a chapter full of what I like to call "investment cooking." It's batch cooking that you can do once a week, or even once a month in some cases, which will mean you have a freezer or fridge full of nourishing, cheap, home-cooked beans, snacks, grains, and treats. It's this cooking that is the backbone of how I cook these days—a little time

one day a week yields enough chickpeas for a week's worth of stews and hummus, and they taste so much better. I find this type of cooking so satisfying, in that it lets me know, for example, that I have a homemade sweet treat I can snack on when I hit a low at 4 p.m. rather than reaching for a cookie.

There is also a chapter on my quick desserts and sweet treats, such as a 10-minute frying-pan crumble, as well as some really easy breakfasts that will make great starts to the day—interesting flavors that come together quickly and make the most of my favorite meal.

This way of cooking is all about simplifying the process, and to some of you that might sound really obvious. More often than not, when I ask people why a recipe hasn't worked, they reply that they burned the onions while they were digging out the coriander seeds from the back of the cupboard, or something along those lines. The only way to cook speedy dinners and stay calm is to be organized up front. I am sure all my friends will read this and laugh, as I have a reputation for being less than well-organized, but in the kitchen I am like a general. The kitchen is my realm and I know that the only way I can cook speedily is to be ordered, organized, and calm, and work through the flow of jobs.

I think of cooking in this way as a practice. It's organized, calm, and has a flow. It's not speedy, hectic stuff. It's just about getting things right, so that you can enjoy every brilliant moment of the alchemy that happens as you turn a pile of ingredients into an incredible offering for you and your family.

So your kitchen needs to be ready to cook in this way. By this, I don't mean you have to buy loads

of expensive equipment. You just need to have an artillery of simple tools that are accessible (see pages 20–21).

I find it really useful to have my ingredients organized too, so that I can find them easily and so that getting ready to cook doesn't mean half an hour of emptying out the entire spice cupboard. I use little glass jars for my spices and keep them on a shelf within reach of the stove, which makes things a lot simpler.

You'll also need a bit of space to cook in. My kitchen counters, like most other people's, can get cluttered, so before I settle down to cook something, I make sure I clear enough space to comfortably cook in. There are a few bits of equipment that can really help speed things up. You'll be fine if you just have the basics, but if you are, for instance, a particularly slow chopper, a food processor will be a great addition to your kitchen. Equally, if you find things keep sticking or burning, maybe it's time for some new pans. All this equipment is a massive investment in cooking from scratch, and that's the best decision we can make for our happiness and our bodies.

When you are ready to cook, start by reading the recipe from top to bottom so that you know what happens when, and how things need to be chopped and cooked. Then put all the equipment you are going to need close by, and get all your ingredients together near your chopping board so that you have everything on hand before you start chopping. These steps are the key to quick, calm cooking and they may sound glaringly obvious, but I have to remind myself to do them every time I cook.

Other clever chef's tricks that make my cooking more speedy are having a mixing bowl on the work surface for peelings and trimmings, so you don't have to keep running back and forth to the trash or compost bin, as well as making sure as much as possible that the area you are working in is close to the stove, so you can do a few jobs at once.

I'm going to ask you to cook on high heat, but don't be afraid of it. Just keep checking things as they cook. I am also going to ask you to preheat your pans to get some serious heat on things that need it, and to use your kettle to speed things up. The kettle is my best friend in the kitchen, and working with boiling water rather than cold from the tap makes everything that much quicker.

This might all sound somewhat hectic, but I believe that making these changes in your kitchen will actually have the opposite effect. You will learn to cook in a way that is calm and choreographed, moving quickly but smoothly through recipes.

And that's what cooking is for me—food that is flavor-packed, nourishing, and not too fussy, and that can be on your table in a reasonable amount of time. It's about using the time you have, however short, to make the tastiest and most delicious dinners possible. In making the most of your time, the incredible ingredients that are in season, and the foods that make you feel good, you can live vibrantly and eat well.

annajones.co.uk
@we_are_food

# Equipment
## for quick cooking

There are a few pieces of equipment I rely on in the kitchen. They range from really cheap to a bit more expensive, but once you have invested in a few of them, you'll be able to make anything in a life-friendly amount of time.

**Y AND JULIENNE PEELERS** My Y peeler has to be the most used gadget in my kitchen and the cheapest. I use it for peeling and for making vegetable ribbons for salads and noodles. I also use a julienne peeler to make noodles from vegetables such as zucchini; it does the job of the currently popular Spiralizer but takes up much less kitchen space. My favorites are the all-metal ones.

**GOOD FRYING PANS** A good frying pan will last a lifetime. I have a good nonstick pan in two sizes, 9 inches and 10 inches, as well as a heavy cast-iron frying pan and a griddle pan. My favorites are GreenPan (which uses a nontoxic ceramic coating) and de Buyer.

**A LARGE SAUCEPAN/STOCKPOT** I make a vat of soup or stock or chickpeas every week, and a large pot makes things much easier. It need not be expensive but it will allow you to cook batches big enough to last a week or fill the freezer. A heavy-bottomed cast-iron one would be my choice, from Le Creuset, but any large, sturdy pan will do.

**STACKABLE GLASS JARS** One of the things that makes a huge difference in my kitchen is having everything accessible and easy to find. I stack all my spices in small glass jars on a shelf next to my stove, which means they are always at hand. I also keep my dry ingredients in large jars for easy access.

**BOX GRATER AND FINE MICROPLANE GRATERS** I use these every day. A good sturdy box grater should set you back between $10 and $15 and is great for grating cheese and vegetables. Microplanes are more sophisticated and a bit more expensive, but one will last a lifetime and they are invaluable for zesting citrus and finely grating garlic, chiles, ginger, or any hard cheese.

**GOOD KNIVES AND A GOOD KNIFE SHARPENER** The main barrier to cooking quickly is being a slow chopper—and how good you are at chopping is directly related to how good and sharp your knives are. I use four main knives in the kitchen: a small chef's knife (about 5 inches), a small serrated paring knife (for tomatoes and fruit), a larger chef's knife (about 8 inches) for sturdy vegetables such as pumpkin or squash, and a good serrated bread knife. I also have a sharpening stone to keep them nice and sharp. My favorite knives are Kin knives, which aren't the cheapest, but you can find knives that are much more expensive. They stay nice and sharp and last a lifetime. I like Opinel for small serrated paring knives, which are very affordable.

**HIGH-SPEED BLENDER**   I use my blender every day for smoothies, soups, nut butters, and hummus. The king of blenders is the Vitamix, which has a super-high-speed motor and will make nuts into butter in a matter of seconds. They are very expensive, though, so I am not going to suggest you all run out and buy one, but they are a great investment if you spend a lot of time in the kitchen. Alternatively, most appliance brands make good sturdy blenders at varying prices—go for the best you can afford.

**FOOD PROCESSOR**   It may seem like overkill to have a food processor and a blender, but they really do different jobs. A blender will liquefy things whereas a food processor will chop and crush things and, if you buy one with some attachments, it can grate and slice too, as well as mix up icings and cake batters. If I can encourage you to buy one thing for your kitchen, it would be a food processor. I have had my Magimix for the last twelve years and it's still going strong. Magimixes have a good range of attachments and are really sturdy, but other brands such as KitchenAid make good food processors too. Again, you get what you pay for here; I would suggest investing as much as you can afford.

**HAND BLENDER**   If you can't get your hands on a blender or a food processor, or your kitchen is too small for big pieces of equipment, then a decent hand blender will stand in for most things. You will need a bit more elbow grease and patience, but it will do the job. I use my hand blender for making dressings and quick pestos and for blending soups, and I find it really useful. Hand blenders come pretty cheap and I use a basic $12 one that has been with me for years.

**KITCHEN SCISSORS**   A good sharp pair of kitchen scissors is always at hand in my kitchen for opening packages and doing little jobs. If you aren't the fastest at chopping with a knife, then chopping small things like herbs or spring onions can be done pretty quickly with a pair of scissors.

## A few notes on ingredients

**COCONUT OIL**   I use coconut oil, which has a mild flavor and a higher smoking point than many other oils, so less nutrients are damaged when it's heated. I recommend coconut oil in many of the recipes in this book. If it's not for you, though, you can generally use a plain olive oil in its place.

**EXTRA-VIRGIN GHEE**   I use ghee (clarified butter) in place of butter. It's basically butter without the whey, and it's full of nutrients such as vitamins A, D, E, and K. It has a high smoking point, keeps for months, and tastes amazing.

**OLIVE OIL**   I keep two types in my kitchen: plain for gentle frying and a flavor-packed extra virgin for dressing and finishing. The extra-virgin one never sees the heat, as it has a low smoke point and creates harmful free radicals if heated too much.

**EGGS**   The eggs I use throughout the recipes are medium eggs, and I always use free-range and organic eggs. If you are vegan, in most of the baking in this book, eggs can be replaced with 1 tablespoon of chia seeds mixed with 3 tablespoons of water, set aside until it forms a gel.

**SALT**   I use British flake sea salt—my favorite is Halen Môn from Anglesey, which has a Protected Designation of Origin status so you know it's from water from Wales (not imported salt rediluted).

**SWEET STUFF**   I keep several natural sweeteners on hand. It is important to remember that while they are higher in nutrients than white sugar, all of these are sugars, so should be used sparingly. Natural sweeteners do tend to be more expensive, so you may want to go for one at a time. I keep these on rotation in my house: maple syrup, honey, agave, coconut sugar, and coconut nectar.

CONGRATULATIONS.

in the
time
it takes
to set
the table

These recipes are for the days and nights when time is shortest and hunger is at its highest. We can all spare fifteen minutes to get dinner on the table. These are ready in the time it takes for the table to be set and are packed with flavor: killer one-pot pastas, quick salads, herb-stuffed omelets, brightly colored speedy soups, piled-high sandwiches, and super-easy quesadillas.

kale, tomato, and lemon magic one-pot spaghetti · tomato, miso, and sesame soup · spiced pea and paneer flatbreads · soft green herb omelet · too hot salad · 10 favorite omelet fillings · gently spiced sweet potato and quinoa bowls · smoky pepper and white bean quesadillas · green pea and coconut soup · pour-over soup · at-your-desk salads · two favorite sandwiches · avocado, tahini, and olive smash flatbreads · avocado, cucumber, and fennel soup

# Kale, tomato, and lemon magic one-pot spaghetti

This pasta is a complete revelation. The sauce is magically made from the pasta water and tomatoes as the pasta cooks—all in one pan. No fuss, one pan, and a killer bowl of pasta.

Pasta and gluten sometimes get bad press. I think there is a time and place for a good bowl of pasta. Saying that, I opt for interesting pastas as often as I do the traditional kind. Try corn, chickpea, or buckwheat spaghetti— they are gluten-free, and all have incredible individual flavors and make a welcome change if pasta is a staple in your house.

The key to this recipe is to measure your water carefully and to use the right pan: you need a large, shallow sauté pan or casserole large enough to fit the pasta lying down. A large, deep frying pan or wok would work well too.

........................................................................................................

Fill and boil a kettle of water and get all your ingredients and equipment together. You need a large, shallow pan with a lid.

Put the pasta into the pan. Quickly chop the tomatoes in half and throw them into the pan. Grate in the zest of both lemons and add the oil and salt. Add about 1 quart/1 liter of boiling water, put a lid on the pan, and bring back to a boil. Remove the lid and simmer on high heat for 6 minutes, using a pair of tongs to turn the pasta every 30 seconds or so as it cooks.

Meanwhile, remove any tough stalks from the kale or spinach and coarsely tear the leaves. Once the pasta has had 6 minutes, add the kale and continue to cook for a further 2 minutes.

Once almost all the water has evaporated, take the pan off the heat and tangle the pasta into four bowls. If you like, top with a little Parmesan.

SERVES 4 GENEROUSLY

14 ounces/400 g spaghetti or linguine

14 ounces/400 g cherry tomatoes

zest of 2 large unwaxed lemons

7 tablespoons/100 ml olive oil

2 heaping teaspoons flaky sea salt (if you are using fine-grain table salt, add a bit less)

1 (14-ounce/400-g) bunch of kale or spinach

Parmesan cheese (I use a vegetarian one) (optional)

# Tomato, miso, and sesame soup

This soup comes together in the time it would take for you to run out to the store for a can of cream of tomato, but it is much more satisfying and full of goodness. It is a clean, fresh tomato soup—the quick cooking keeps the flavor perky and bright. I add miso and tahini here, which are two of my favorite partners for tomatoes, the earthy creaminess of the tahini and the deep saltiness of the miso backing up the clean tomato flavor like a dream. In the winter, when fresh tomatoes aren't at their best, you could use two 14-ounce/400-g cans of tomatoes and forget the fresh ones.

I have suggested a quick topping to take this soup to the next level in flavor terms. If you are really pushed for time, some chopped cilantro would suffice.

..........................................................................................................................

Fill and boil a kettle of water and get all your ingredients and equipment together. Put a large pan over low heat.

Working quickly, chop the green onions and add them to the pan with a splash of coconut or olive oil. Turn up the heat to medium and stir from time to time for a couple of minutes until beginning to brown. Chop the fresh tomatoes in half (bigger ones into quarters) and add them to the pan. Add the canned tomatoes, fill the can with boiling water and pour this in too, then add the miso and bring to a boil.

Meanwhile, make the topping. Mix the honey, tahini, miso, and lemon juice in a bowl and put to one side. Toast the sesame seeds in a dry frying pan until golden, and chop the cilantro.

Once the soup has come to a boil, it's done. Take it off the heat, add the tahini, and blend well with a handheld blender, adding a little salt if needed. The sweetness of tomatoes, the salty depth of miso, and the creamy earthiness of tahini should be well balanced. Ladle into four bowls and top with the miso and honey mixture, the sesame seeds, and some chopped cilantro.

SERVES 4

4 green onions
coconut or olive oil
17 ounces/500 g vine-ripened tomatoes
1 (14-ounce/400-g) can of chopped tomatoes
2 tablespoons miso paste (I use a dark barley miso)
1 tablespoon tahini
sea salt

FOR THE TOPPING (OPTIONAL)
1 tablespoon runny honey
1 tablespoon tahini
1 tablespoon miso paste
juice of ½ lemon
4 tablespoons sesame seeds
a small bunch of cilantro

# Spiced pea and paneer flatbreads

These are super-quick and flavor-packed, and they're what I make when I want some serious flavors but don't have much time. Here, sweet lemon-spiked peas are mashed and piled onto warm flatbreads, then topped with crispy cauliflower and heady spices. Finish with a little crispy paneer (I show you how to make paneer on page 248) if you like.

Fill and boil a kettle of water and get all your ingredients and equipment together. Put a griddle pan over high heat.

Finely slice the green onions, put into a pan with a little coconut oil, and fry over medium heat until just turning golden. Put the peas into a heatproof mixing bowl, pour boiling water over them, and leave for 5 minutes.

Chop the cauliflower into small florets and add to the green onion pan with the curry leaves and spices. Cook for 2 to 3 minutes, until the cauliflower has lost its rawness and is coated with the spices, then turn the heat up, squeeze over the juice of 1 lemon and allow to evaporate, then take off the heat.

Chop the green chile and the stalks of the cilantro (put the cilantro leaves aside). Drain the peas and mash with the zest of the other lemon and half its juice, the green chile, cilantro stalks, and a good pinch of salt and pepper.

If you are using the paneer, transfer the cauliflower to a bowl and put the pan back on the heat. Add a little coconut oil and, once it's really hot, crumble in the paneer; cook over high heat for a minute or two, until the cheese crisps up.

Warm the flatbreads in a dry pan or over a gas flame until warm and crisped at the edges. Top with the pea mash, the cauliflower, and the crispy paneer, then chop the mint and the cilantro leaves and scatter over the top.

**MAKES 4 FLATBREADS**

a small bunch of green onions
coconut oil
9 ounces/250 g frozen peas
1 small cauliflower
a small handful of curry leaves
2 teaspoons mustard seeds
1 teaspoon ground turmeric
2 unwaxed lemons
1 green chile
a small bunch of cilantro
sea salt and freshly ground pepper
5 ounces/150 g paneer (optional)
4 flatbreads
a small bunch of mint

# Soft green herb omelet

This is what I make when reserves are low in every sense of the word, and it's a great way to use up the last bits of a few bunches of herbs.

Omelets are my ultimate quick dinner and one of my favorite meals— you can put a perfect one on the table in under 15 minutes. For lots more ideas on how to put them together, see pages 34 and 35. I make my omelets soft and curdy and just set, and I like them simply spiked with a generous amount of heady soft herbs. Sometimes I skip any filling, as I like the clean simplicity, and I serve mine with a shock of peppery arugula in a punchy vinaigrette.

You can use whatever soft herbs you have on hand—my favorite combination is basil, mint, dill, and tarragon. The quality of eggs you use here is absolutely key: there is no hiding, and you want the best you can get your hands on—organic or pastured eggs with paint-pot-yellow yolks.

SERVES 2

4 free-range or organic eggs
sea salt and freshly ground pepper
2 small bunches of soft herbs,
a mix of any of the following:
mint, parsley, dill, chives, tarragon,
chervil, basil
a little butter or coconut oil

FOR THE FILLING
a small handful of goat, feta,
or ricotta cheese
a good grating of lemon zest
(from an unwaxed lemon)
a handful of shredded spinach
or other greens

TO SERVE
a couple of handfuls of arugula
or watercress in vinaigrette
chopped dill

Get all your ingredients and equipment together. You need a large nonstick frying pan.

Crack your eggs into a bowl, add a healthy pinch of salt and a good bit of pepper, and whisk with a fork. Finely chop all the herbs and add them to the eggs.

Heat your frying pan over medium heat and once it's hot, add the butter or oil, allow it to bubble, then lift and tilt the pan so the butter covers the surface.

Put the pan back on the burner and then, with the fork still nearby, pour the eggs into the pan and allow them to sit untouched for 20 seconds or so, until they begin to set. Now use the fork to pull the omelet away from the edge

CONTINUED

of the pan into the middle, angling the pan so the egg runs back into the bit you have just exposed. Do this another five or six times in different places so you have undulating waves of sunshine-yellow egg. Now leave your omelet to cook until it is almost set, which should take a minute or two.

If you are going to fill your omelet, now is the time. Scatter the fillings on one half of the omelet, then flip the other side over to form a half-moon shape, and cook for another 30 seconds.

Your omelet should be just set in the middle, still soft and curdy, just turning golden in patches on the outside. Once it's perfect, slide the omelet out of the pan onto a warm plate and serve immediately with a shock of dressed salad.

# Too hot salad

I make this when it feels too hot to eat or I am in need of something a bit refreshing. I first made it on a humid summer's day in London, one of those hot city days when the air doesn't move and all you can think about is swimming pools and popsicles. Now every time I make this I start singing Kool and the Gang songs.

The key here is to get everything nice and cold. Search out raw red-skinned peanuts if you can. In the summer I soak a few handfuls in cold water overnight and keep them cool in the fridge for snacking. They are also great in stir-fries and on top of morning fruit. They are fresh and juicy and completely different from roasted peanuts. You can easily find them in health food stores or Indian groceries.

For a heartier meal, serve this with cooked and cooled brown basmati rice or some thin rice vermicelli noodles.

.................................................................................................................

Get all your ingredients and equipment together. Soak the peanuts in ice water and put them into the fridge while you get on with everything else.

Peel the carrots, then use a Y peeler to peel them into long strips and place them in a bowl with some ice water.

Cut the watermelon into bite-size pieces, removing any very seedy parts and the outer skin. Halve the cherry tomatoes. Pop both into a serving bowl and put into the fridge.

Use the Y peeler to peel the cucumber into long strips, stopping when you get to the watery seeded part, and add to the serving bowl of watermelon and tomatoes in the fridge. Shred the lettuce and pick the cilantro leaves from the stalks.

CONTINUED

SERVES 4

1¾ ounces/50 g raw peanuts
(see headnote)
2 carrots
7 ounces/200 g watermelon
a handful of cherry tomatoes
1 cucumber
1 Little Gem or romaine lettuce
head, or ½ a head of iceberg
a bunch of cilantro

FOR THE DRESSING
½ red chile
1 tablespoon soy sauce or tamari
2 limes
a little runny honey

To make the dressing, chop the red chile and put into a small bowl with the soy, the juice of both limes, and a small squeeze of honey. Taste and adjust, adding more lime, honey, and soy if needed until you have a nice balance of heat, acidity, and sweetness.

Take the serving bowl and the peanuts out of the fridge. Drain the peanuts and carrots well, add to the serving bowl and pour over the dressing. Toss with the lettuce and scatter over the cilantro. Eat in a breezy spot, while thinking of dipping your feet in the pool.

# 10 favorite omelet fillings

An omelet is one of the ultimate quick dinners. These are my 10 favorite omelet fillings, but follow this pattern and you can't go wrong: main vegetable, backup vegetable, accent flavor, backup flavor, richness.

See page 28 for my favorite way to make an omelet, and remember to buy the best eggs you can.

| | **MAIN VEGETABLE** → | **BACKUP VEGETABLE** → |
|---|---|---|
| 1 | Sauté 3½ ounces/100 g of spinach | With 2 ounces/50 g of halved cherry tomatoes |
| 2 | Slice a red onion and sauté until soft | Add a handful of shredded greens |
| 3 | Fry some sliced leftover potatoes | With a few roasted red peppers from a jar |
| 4 | Sauté 3½ ounces/100 g of greens | Add ½ a mashed avocado |
| 5 | Sauté a handful of mushrooms | With a handful of spinach |
| 6 | Finely slice and sauté some asparagus | With 1 finely sliced zucchini |
| 7 | Sauté some grated winter squash | With a handful of cooked chickpeas |
| 8 | Cook a handful of peas | With a handful of fava beans |
| 9 | Sauté a grated carrot | With a handful of chopped mint |
| 10 | Slice 1 small leek and sauté until soft | Add a handful of mushrooms |

| ACCENT FLAVOR → | BACKUP FLAVOR → | RICHNESS |
|---|---|---|
| Add a few basil leaves | Add 1 ounce/25 g of toasted pine nuts | Finish with a good grating of pecorino |
| Add the leaves from 2 sprigs of thyme | Add a splash of balsamic vinegar | Add a crumbling of goat cheese |
| Add a handful of chopped parsley | Add a good pinch of smoked paprika | Add a grating of Manchego |
| Add a few torn basil leaves | Add the zest and juice of ½ a lemon | Finish with a crumbling of feta |
| Add ½ a chopped chile | Add the juice of a lemon | Finish with a grating of Parmesan |
| Mix in a tablespoon of pesto | Grate in the zest of ½ a lemon | And a little crumble of goat cheese |
| Add a teaspoon of harissa | Grate in the zest of a lemon | Add a final crumbling of feta |
| Add a small handful of chopped mint | Squeeze in the juice of ½ a lemon | Add a good drizzle of olive oil |
| Stir in some toasted almonds | Squeeze in the juice of ½ a lemon | Top with a crumbling of feta or paneer |
| Add the leaves from a few sprigs of tarragon or dill | Add a teaspoon of mustard | Add a small handful of grated cheddar |

# Gently spiced sweet potato and quinoa bowls

The first time we made this was one of those moments where a few things pulled out of the fridge were thrown together for a quick dinner and the stars aligned to make something brilliant. It is, in fact, my partner John's recipe. He is amazing at cooking quick, nutritious food, and is about the only person I know who really truly honestly in his heart of hearts would prefer a bowl of vegetables to just about anything else.

You can have this on your table in about 15 minutes; it uses quinoa in a way I would never have considered, yet it is so good. Here, coconut and turmeric are backed up by minerally greens and a final shock of lemon. Good, quick, tasty eating.

I use chard, but spinach would work just fine. Creamed coconut used instead of coconut milk gives a more intense flavor and lends itself well to quick cooking.

SERVES 3

1 cup/150 g quinoa

1 teaspoon vegetable stock powder, or ½ stock cube

4 green onions

1 clove garlic

coconut oil

2 teaspoons mustard seeds (I use black)

2 carrots

1 sweet potato

½ (7-ounce/200-g) package of creamed coconut

1 teaspoon ground turmeric

½ (14-ounce/400-g) can of chickpeas, or 1½ cups/ 250 g home-cooked chickpeas (see pages 241–245)

sea salt

1 (14-ounce/400-g) bunch of chard

1 lemon

Fill and boil a kettle of water and get all your ingredients and equipment together.

Weigh out the quinoa in a mug or measuring cup, making note of the level it comes up to, quickly rinse it with cold water, then pour it into a large saucepan. Fill the mug to the same level with boiling water and add to the pan, then repeat so you have double the volume of water as quinoa. Add the stock powder or cube, then put the pan over high heat, put the lid on, and cook the quinoa at a steady simmer for 10 to 12 minutes, until almost all the water has been absorbed and the little curly grain has been released from each quinoa seed.

Meanwhile, chop the green onions into thin rounds. Peel and finely slice the garlic. Put a saucepan over medium heat and add a dollop of coconut oil.

CONTINUED

Throw in the green onions and cook for a couple of minutes, then add the garlic and the mustard seeds and cook until the seeds begin to pop.

Peel the carrots and cut in half lengthwise and then into thin slices, then do the same with the sweet potato. It's important that the slices are thin, so that the vegetables cook quickly. Add them to the pan and cook for a minute before adding the creamed coconut, turmeric, drained chickpeas, 1⅔ cups/400 ml of hot water and a good pinch of salt. Bring to a boil and simmer for 5 minutes, until the sweet potato is soft.

Keep an eye on your quinoa—it should have absorbed all the water by now, and the little curly grains should be visible. If they are, turn off the heat and leave the lid on.

Finally, cut the leaves off the chard and shred them finely, then finely slice the stalks. Heat a tiny bit of coconut oil in a frying pan, add the stalks and sauté for a minute, then add the leaves and sauté until wilted—this will take 2 to 3 minutes.

Once the sweet potato is cooked, stir the quinoa into the coconut and sweet potato. Serve in deep bowls, with the chard on top, and finish with a squeeze of lemon.

# Smoky pepper and white bean quesadillas

Quesadillas get a bad rap for being cheese-laden and heavy, but they are a truly quick meal, and when filled with more than cheese, they become more nourishing and much more delicious.

Here I have stepped away from straight-up Mexican quesadillas and introduced some Spanish flavors. Roasted red peppers, smoky paprika, and white beans—it makes me think of summer trips to Barcelona, and that can never be a bad thing.

If you are vegan, leave the cheese out and double the white beans, which hold it all together; you may want to be more generous with the seasoning too. I mostly make these at lunchtime, but they are filling enough for a dinner— you might want some sherry vinegar–dressed green salad on the side.

If you are making these for a party, which I often do, the filling can be made in bigger batches really easily. The quesadillas can be stacked in the fridge, filled and ready for cooking.

SERVES 2 (MAKES 1 DEEPLY FILLED QUESADILLA)

2 green onions

olive oil

½ teaspoon smoked paprika

¼ cup/50 g cooked white beans

⅔ cup/100 g jarred roasted red peppers

1 unwaxed lemon

½ bunch of parsley

1¾ ounces/50 g Manchego cheese

2 whole wheat or seeded tortillas or wraps

a handful of cherry tomatoes

Get all your ingredients together.

Finely slice the green onions. Put a frying pan over medium heat, add a little olive oil, the green onions, and smoked paprika, and cook for a couple of minutes, until starting to brown.

Meanwhile, put the white beans into a mixing bowl and mash them with a fork, then coarsely chop your red peppers and add half of them to the beans. Grate over the zest of the lemon, then coarsely chop the parsley and add half to the bowl. Grate in your Manchego. Once the green onions are browned, add these too.

CONTINUED

Lay a tortilla or wrap on your work surface. Spoon the red pepper mixture all over it, spread it evenly, then top with the other tortilla. Heat a frying pan and toast the quesadilla for a couple of minutes on each side—
I do this dry, but you can add a splash of oil if you like your quesadillas crispy. If you find it hard to flip, a plate on top might help.

While the quesadilla is toasting, coarsely chop the tomatoes, mix with the remaining peppers and parsley, and squeeze in the juice of half the lemon.

Once the quesadilla is toasted on both sides, remove it from the pan and cut into six pieces. Serve in the middle of the table, with the salsa for spooning over.

# Green pea and coconut soup

When I am hungry and impatient and I have nothing in the fridge, this simple soup is the recipe I turn to.

For a really speedy soup, the pan you use is important; a small, deep saucepan will mean your soup won't come to a simmer quickly, so I suggest a deep, wide saucepan. Cast iron is ideal as it conducts the heat evenly, so even though you are cooking quickly it's less likely that your soup will catch on the bottom. Of course use what you have, but a good, deep, heavy-bottomed saucepan is a great investment.

If you don't have green onions, a normal onion will do fine—you may just need to cook it for a little longer.

....................................................................................................................................

Fill and boil a kettle of water and get all your ingredients and equipment together. Put a large soup pan, one that has a lid, over medium heat to warm up.

Chop the green onions quite finely and put into the pan with the coconut oil. Turn up the heat to its highest and cook for 2 minutes, until softened.

Add the peas to the pan with the coconut milk, the stock powder, and 3 cups/750 ml of boiling water, then put a lid on and bring to a boil. Once it's boiling, simmer, still over high heat, for 2 to 3 minutes.

Take off the heat. Add most of the herbs, stalks and all, and the juice of the lemon and use a handheld blender to puree the soup until super-smooth.

Ladle into bowls and top with a little olive oil and the rest of the herbs.

SERVES 4 TO 6

a bunch of green onions
1 teaspoon coconut oil
2 pounds/1 kg frozen peas
1 (14-ounce/400-ml) can of coconut milk
1 tablespoon vegetable stock powder or ½ stock cube
a bunch of basil or cilantro (or a mixture of both)
1 lemon

TO SERVE
extra-virgin olive oil

# Pour-over soup

This soup is the epitome of quick cooking. Finely sliced vegetables, delicate noodles, and flavor-packed aromatics all come together to make a soup that's ready in the time it takes to boil the kettle. Most of the cooking is done by adding the boiling water from the kettle, so no pans, just a couple of bowls and a bit of chopping.

You can mix and match the veggies you use here for variety, but just make sure they are ones that will be edible with very little cooking—greens, finely sliced carrots, grated winter squash, and sliced mushrooms all work well.

This is a great, healthy meal to take to work if that's your thing; just keep it in the fridge and pour over the hot water at your desk.

Fill and boil a kettle of water and get all your ingredients out. You'll need two heatproof mixing bowls with a plate that fits on top.

Once the kettle has boiled, put the noodles into one of the mixing bowls and cover with boiling water. Leave to sit, covered with a plate.

Peel the ginger and grate into the other bowl, then add the creamed coconut, white miso, sesame oil, soy, and star anise. Very finely slice the green onion and the chile and add most of them to the bowl. Shred the greens, cut the zucchini into thin slices and slice the sugar snaps. Add them all to the bowl.

Once the noodles have had 3 minutes, drain them and add them to the bowl of green veggies. If you're making the soup for lunch later, layer everything into a screwtop jar and finish the recipe when you're ready to eat. Reboil the kettle. Pour hot water from the kettle over the noodles and veggies until they are just covered, and mix well.

Garnish with the remaining chopped green onion and chile, a little basil or cilantro, and the toasted sesame seeds.

SERVES 1

1¾ ounces/50 g thin rice vermicelli (I use brown rice ones)
a small piece of ginger
1 tablespoon creamed coconut
a good spoonful of white miso paste
a splash of sesame oil
1 tablespoon soy sauce or tamari
1 star anise
1 green onion
1 red chile
a small handful of greens
½ a zucchini
a small handful of sugar snap peas

TO SERVE
a few sprigs of basil or cilantro
1 tablespoon toasted sesame seeds

# at-your-desk salads

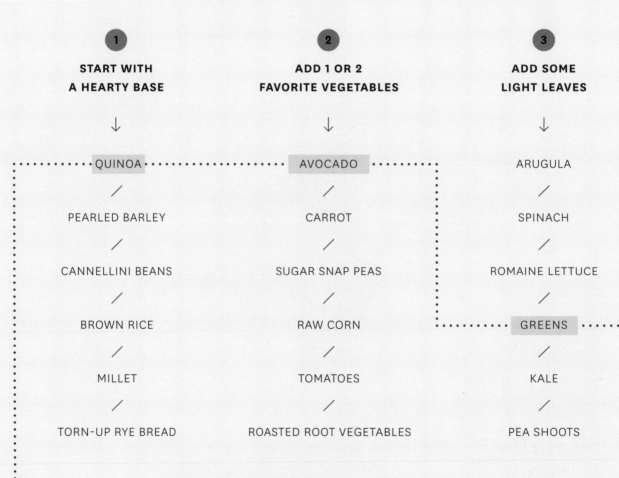

| **1** | **2** | **3** |
|---|---|---|
| **START WITH A HEARTY BASE** | **ADD 1 OR 2 FAVORITE VEGETABLES** | **ADD SOME LIGHT LEAVES** |
| ↓ | ↓ | ↓ |
| QUINOA | AVOCADO | ARUGULA |
| PEARLED BARLEY | CARROT | SPINACH |
| CANNELLINI BEANS | SUGAR SNAP PEAS | ROMAINE LETTUCE |
| BROWN RICE | RAW CORN | GREENS |
| MILLET | TOMATOES | KALE |
| TORN-UP RYE BREAD | ROASTED ROOT VEGETABLES | PEA SHOOTS |

EXAMPLE

Lunch on the run or at your desk can be dull and monotonous. Use this guide to make your own quick salads. Using a grain or legume as a base will mean it is filling, and its hardiness means your salad will travel well.

Take one element from each column and stack in a wide jar or plastic containers, making sure you work in layers from the heaviest (grains) to the lightest (leaves).

Make a dressing in a small jam jar, or pour it into a small bowl lined with plastic wrap, bring the ends together and twist to make a little dressing package. I mix one of the suggested dressing flavors with 1 tablespoon of olive oil, a good squeeze of lemon juice, salt, and pepper. The nutrition from salad leaves is actually boosted when we dress them, as the good fat from the oil makes it easier for our bodies to take up the nutrients.

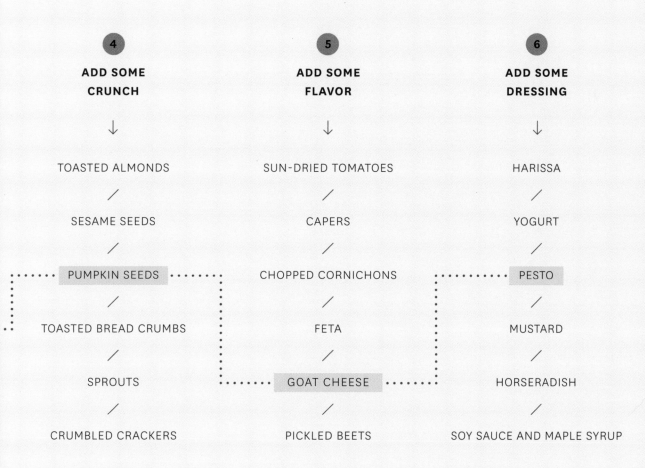

**4**

**ADD SOME
CRUNCH**

↓

TOASTED ALMONDS

/

SESAME SEEDS

/

PUMPKIN SEEDS

/

TOASTED BREAD CRUMBS

/

SPROUTS

/

CRUMBLED CRACKERS

**5**

**ADD SOME
FLAVOR**

↓

SUN-DRIED TOMATOES

/

CAPERS

/

CHOPPED CORNICHONS

/

FETA

/

GOAT CHEESE

/

PICKLED BEETS

**6**

**ADD SOME
DRESSING**

↓

HARISSA

/

YOGURT

/

PESTO

/

MUSTARD

/

HORSERADISH

/

SOY SAUCE AND MAPLE SYRUP

# Two favorite sandwiches

Sandwiches are unbeatable. They are super quick, usually pretty cheap, and as long as you get yourself some good bread and stuff the sandwiches with a few vegetables, they can be super good for you too.

Everyone has their favorite sandwich; these are the two that are made most in my kitchen. Both require five minutes' work but you'll be glad you took the extra time. These recipes have been written for one sandwich but can easily be scaled up for more. They both work really well on rye bread too.

## KALE SMASH, HONEYED CARROT, AND HUMMUS

MAKES 1 SANDWICH

a handful of kale
2 sun-dried tomatoes
1 lemon
extra-virgin olive oil
sea salt and freshly ground pepper
1 small carrot
a little squeeze of honey
2 slices of good sourdough bread
1 tablespoon hummus
a handful of lettuce leaves, shredded
(I use Little Gem)

Get all your ingredients together.

Put the kale into a food processor with the sun-dried tomatoes, a squeeze of lemon juice, a tablespoon of olive oil, and a pinch of salt and pepper. Process until you have a paste.

Next, peel and finely slice the carrot, put it into a pan with the honey, a little olive oil, salt, and pepper, and cook over medium heat until just softened and not too crunchy.

Toast your bread, then spread one slice thickly with kale smash and one with hummus. Put the carrots on top of the hummus, add the shredded lettuce, and sandwich together.

**SAGE AND LEMON PESTO, PECORINO, AND HONEY**

......................................................................................................................

FOR THE QUICK SAGE PESTO

3½ ounces/100 g raw almonds
(preferably soaked)

zest of 1 unwaxed lemon and
half its juice

2 sprigs of sage

a pinch of sea salt

2 tablespoons extra-virgin olive oil

sea salt and freshly ground pepper

2 slices of multigrain
or sourdough bread

1¾ ounces/50 g pecorino cheese
(I use a vegetarian one)

1 teaspoon thick honey

extra-virgin olive oil

Get all your ingredients together.

First make your sage pesto. In a food processor, blend all the ingredients until you have a chunky pesto, and season with more salt and pepper to taste.

Heat a frying pan over medium heat. Slather one slice of bread thickly with sage pesto, then slice the pecorino thinly and lay it on top (store the remaining pesto in a small jar in the refrigerator). Spread the honey on the other slice and sandwich together. Drizzle the outsides of the sandwich with a little olive oil, then put into the pan and toast on both sides until golden, using a spatula to press down as needed.

Once the sandwich is toasted and golden, cut in half and devour.

# Avocado, tahini, and olive smash flatbreads

I try to sneak avocados in anywhere I can. I love their buttery, grassy, rich creaminess. Avocado on toast was something I grew up on, and my love of avos has undoubtedly been inherited from my mum.

So I thought it was time to mix things up a bit, still making the most of how instantly delicious an avocado is but adding some more unusual flavors. Here I smash avocados with tahini, olives, and lemon to make one of my new favorite lunches.

This is equally good on toast. I often double the recipe and serve it in bowls with homemade tortilla chips, to make an amazing snack for a crowd.

SERVES 2 AS A LUNCH
OR 4 AS A SNACK

2 ripe avocados
sea salt and freshly ground pepper
½ lemon
1 clementine or ½ orange
2 tablespoons tahini
2 handfuls of Kalamata olives
½ small clove garlic

TO SERVE
4 flatbreads or tortillas
red chile flakes
toasted cumin seeds
fresh green herbs
(I use dill, basil, or parsley)
feta cheese (optional)

Get all your ingredients together.

Halve and pit the avocados and scoop the flesh into a bowl with a good pinch of salt and pepper. Squeeze over the juice of the lemon and the clementine. Add the tahini and coarsely smash and mash until you have a half-smooth, half-chunky mixture. Pit and coarsely chop the olives and add them to the bowl. Very finely chop or grate the garlic and add that to the bowl too. Gently mix to combine.

Heat the flatbreads either in a dry frying pan or over an open gas flame, turning them with tongs once they have browned a little. This will take a few seconds on a gas flame and more like 30 seconds to 1 minute in a pan.

Cut the flatbreads into quarters and pile on the avocado mixture. Top with a scattering of chile flakes, toasted cumin seeds, and a few delicate herbs. If you like, you can add a crumble of feta.

# Avocado, cucumber, and fennel soup

This soup couldn't be easier, and it's one of the quickest recipes I've ever made. It's what I eat on hot days or days when I feel like something light, refreshing, and cleansing. I don't think that this kind of super-fresh food should be banished from the winter, though. I have been known to eat a bowl of this in front of the fire in January after Christmastime overindulging.

I mention using avocado oil here; if you don't have it, a good extra-virgin olive oil will be great, but avocado oil has such an amazing buttery taste that it is worth searching out. Use it anywhere you might use good olive oil, to finish soups, and in dressings.

SERVES 2 AS A MEAL
OR 4 AS A STARTER

1 ripe avocado

1 cucumber

½ large fennel bulb

2 tablespoons Greek
or coconut yogurt

juice of ½ lemon

a handful of ice cubes

sea salt and freshly ground pepper

a few sprigs of dill

a few sprigs of basil

½ green chile

a handful of toasted
pumpkin seeds

extra-virgin olive oil
or avocado oil

Get all your ingredients together.

Pit the avocado and scoop the flesh into the jar of a blender. Chop the cucumber and fennel into large pieces and add these too, along with the yogurt, lemon juice, ice cubes, and a good pinch of salt and pepper. Blend on high until you have a completely smooth pale green soup. Taste the soup and add more lemon or salt if needed; the flavor should be subtle and refreshing, with a back note of lemon.

Once the soup is completely smooth, pour into bowls and top with fronds of dill, little basil leaves, chopped green chile, some pumpkin seeds, and a good drizzle of oil. If it's a really hot day, you can add a couple more ice cubes too.

ready
in twenty

Here are some life-friendly dinners, layered with a rainbow of veggies, for when you have a dash more time. These are hearty meals: generous salads, hash browns, homemade beans, quick-as-a-flash Vietnamese noodles, rainbow goodness bowls, quick stews, vibrant nachos, roasted lemon zucchini, and quick quinoa risotto.

early summer green goddess salad · lima beans with fennel, lemon, and tomato · smoky beans and sweet potato hash browns · kale, sumac, and crispy rice salad · lemongrass, peanut, and herb noodles salad · goodness bowls · plantain, avocado, and black bean bowl · sweet potato, lime, and peanut soup · quick saffron polenta bake · winter root vegetable soba noodles with pickled greens · seeded halloumi and harissa rainbow bowl · green mimosa salad · cashew, kale, and lime nacho bowl · sesame, pistachio, and preserved lemon crispy rice · black-eyed peas with chard and green herb smash · crispy cauliflower rice with sticky spiced cashews · zucchini noodles with pistachio, green herbs, and ricotta · charred broccolini with cucumber noodles and peanut sauce · quinoa risotto with mashed peas and greens · beet and buckwheat pancakes · quick 20-minute stir-fries

# Early summer green goddess salad

Coconuts and avocados are two of my favorite things, and luckily they are a happy pairing. Here they join forces to create an incredible dinner salad as fresh and zippy as it is satisfying. This dressing is inspired by the famous green goddess dressing I loved so much growing up in San Francisco. My version has some coconut milk and a kick from rice wine vinegar and soy.

Search out the ripest avocados, as this salad is really a love song to their creamy, grassy deliciousness. When asparagus isn't around, I make this with purple sprouting broccoli. If I am really hungry I add some cooked and cooled buckwheat noodles, quinoa, or brown rice to my bowl too.

Fill and boil a kettle of water and get all your ingredients and equipment together.

Put a frying pan over high heat. Chop the asparagus stalks into ½-inch/ 1-cm coins, leaving the tips intact. Add a little oil to the pan and add all the asparagus. Cook for a couple of minutes to take off the raw edge, then take the pan off the heat.

Place the sugar snaps in a bowl (I like to cut them in half down the middle, but you can leave them whole to save time) with the edamame. Cover with boiling water and leave to one side.

Now make the dressing. Scoop half an avocado into a blender (or use a deep bowl and an immersion blender). Add the coconut milk, honey, chile, half the basil and cilantro (stalks and all), the soy, and vinegar and blend until smooth and green. Taste, and add more soy, vinegar, or honey, if needed.

Put the spinach into a serving bowl. Drain the sugar snaps and edamame well and add them to the spinach with the asparagus. Cut the avocado in half and take out the pit, then use a knife to criss-cross both halves all the way to the skin. Using a spoon, scoop the avocado flesh into the bowl. Finish by topping with the dressing, the rest of the basil and cilantro, and the sesame seeds.

## SERVES 4

a bunch of asparagus
olive oil
14 ounces/400 g sugar snap peas
10 ounces/300 g edamame
10 ounces/300 g baby spinach
1 ripe avocado
⅓ cup/50 g toasted white or black sesame seeds

### FOR THE DRESSING

½ ripe avocado
4 tablespoons coconut milk
a squeeze of runny honey or agave syrup
1 green chile
a small bunch of basil
a small bunch of cilantro
2 tablespoons light soy sauce or tamari
4 tablespoons rice wine vinegar

# Lima beans with fennel, lemon, and tomato

I buy Greek gigantes beans—tomato-and-dill-spiked buttery beans generously coated in olive oil—in jars from my local shop and feast on them with flatbreads when I'm feeling lazy. This is how I make them at home: as more of a quick stew, with heady lemon, caramelized fennel, and some fennel seeds, which is my nod to the traditional shot of ouzo. I haven't added as much oil as the Greeks often do, but if you like things richer, you can add a generous drizzle at the end. I often serve this with feta, warm flatbreads, and some greens.

SERVES 4

1 large fennel bulb

olive oil

a small bunch of green onions

2 cloves garlic

7 ounces/200 g cherry tomatoes

1 lemon

½ teaspoon fennel seeds

1 tablespoon dried oregano, or a small handful of chopped fresh oregano

a pinch of dried chile flakes

1 tablespoon runny honey

1 tablespoon red wine vinegar

2 (14-ounce/400-g) cans of cooked white beans, or 1½ cups/250 g home-cooked beans (see pages 241–245)

a small bunch of dill

extra-virgin olive oil

First prepare the fennel. Remove the bulb's tough outside layer, then trim and slice along the length of the bulb through the root into ½-inch/1-cm slices.

Heat a large heavy frying pan over medium-high heat and add a good drizzle of olive oil. When the pan is hot and the oil starts to ripple, add the fennel, spreading it out so one flat side hits the pan. Cook for about 2 minutes, until browned and caramelized, then turn over and cook for another 2 minutes. Meanwhile, chop the green onions and garlic. Once the fennel is browned, add the green onions and garlic to the pan and stir for a couple of minutes.

Chop the tomatoes and cut the lemon into wedges, then add both to the pan with the fennel seeds, oregano, chile flakes, honey, and vinegar. Let the liquid heat and reduce for a minute or so before adding the beans and 7 tablespoons/100 ml of water. Cook until the beans are warmed through, about 5 minutes.

Chop the dill and scatter over to finish, along with a good drizzle of olive oil.

# Smoky beans and sweet potato hash browns

Nothing fancy here. Just a good quick dinner, which doubles as a favorite brunch too. If you like, add a fried egg to top it off, or some dressed greens.

If you are vegan or don't eat eggs, you can use 2 tablespoons of chia seeds mixed with 6 tablespoons of water to bind the hash browns instead of the eggs.

.......................................................................................................................................................

Finely chop the shallot, put it into a hot pan with a little oil, and cook for 4 to 5 minutes, until browned.

Meanwhile grate your sweet potatoes into a big mixing bowl, add a good pinch of salt and pepper, the cumin seeds, and the eggs, and mix together well.

When the shallot is beginning to brown, add the smoked paprika and cook for a minute. Coarsely chop the tomatoes and add to the pan, then drain the beans and add these too, along with a splash of balsamic and the leaves from the thyme. Add a good pinch of salt and pepper and cook for 5 minutes, until the sauce has thickened and the tomatoes have broken down.

Heat a little oil in a large frying pan. Divide the sweet potato mixture roughly into four and use your hands to make one quarter into a patty, then carefully put it into the pan to fry. Do this with the rest of the mix, so you have four patties. Cook over low to medium heat for 4 to 6 minutes, until golden brown, then use a thin spatula to carefully flip and cook for another 4 to 6 minutes. As the patties cook, use the spatula to gently push down on them to pack everything together.

Serve the hash browns with the beans.

SERVES 2

1 shallot or ½ red onion

olive oil

2 sweet potatoes (about 17 ounces/500 g)

sea salt and freshly ground pepper

½ teaspoon cumin seeds

2 free-range or organic eggs

½ teaspoon smoked paprika

3½ ounces/100 g cherry tomatoes

1 (14-ounce/400-g) can of cannellini beans

a dash of balsamic vinegar

leaves from a few sprigs of thyme

# Kale, sumac, and crispy rice salad

This is an amazing salad based on one I ate at an incredible neighborhood café in Los Angeles. Sqirl is one of those places where you want every single thing on the menu, right down to the drinks. On my last trip to L.A., I ate there five times. For someone who doesn't like routine, that's pretty solid. This is a play on my favorite thing on the menu. It has inspired flavors (with sumac and lime) and textures (with kale and crispy rice).

I am going to ask you to cook your rice three times here, which may seem crazy, but it'll create perfect little pops of crunch against the rest of the salad. This is a great way to use up leftover rice too—just skip the first cooking stage. It's also really good topped with a softly poached egg or some feta and flatbreads if you are hungry.

Bear in mind that if you use brown rice, it will take about 20 minutes to cook.

.........................................................................................................................

SERVES 4 AS A SIDE OR
2 AS A MAIN DISH

½ cup/100 g basmati rice
(I use brown)

a bunch of curly kale, green
or purple (about 7 ounces/200 g)

zest and juice of 1 unwaxed lemon

sea salt

3 green onions

2 tablespoons coconut oil

FOR THE DRESSING

zest and juice of 1 unwaxed lime

1 tablespoon sumac (optional)

2 tablespoons good olive oil

1 teaspoon runny honey

freshly ground pepper

6 medjool dates

Fill and boil a kettle of water and get all your ingredients and a large frying pan together.

Cook the rice in a small saucepan of boiling salted water until cooked—this will take 10 to 15 minutes.

Meanwhile, pull the kale from its stems and shred the leaves with a knife or tear into small pieces with your hands. Put the leaves into a bowl, then add the zest and juice of the lemon and a good pinch of salt and scrunch it in your hands for a minute to break it down a little. Chop the green onions finely and add them to the bowl.

Once the rice is cooked, drain it well. Put a large frying pan over heat and when it's hot, add the rice with no oil and dry-fry for a couple of minutes to get rid of any moisture.

⁙· CONTINUED

Remove the rice from the pan, then put the pan back on the heat, add half the coconut oil at a time, and fry the rice in two batches until starting to turn lightly brown and really crispy. Drain on paper towels and sprinkle with salt.

Now make your dressing. Put the zest and juice of the lime into a screwtop jar with the sumac, if using, olive oil, honey, and a pinch each of salt and pepper. Put on the lid and shake to combine.

Pit and coarsely chop the dates and add to the kale. Once the rice is almost cool, add it to the kale and toss with the dressing.

# Lemongrass, peanut, and herb noodle salad

You can't live in East London and fail to be inspired by the endless and sometimes brilliant Vietnamese restaurants that line the streets of Hackney. Outside London, though, it's harder to lay your hands on the bright, fresh food I love so much.

This take on *bun cha* is a fragrant, delicate rice noodle salad. I have taken the original Hanoi recipe and made my own chile-spiked tofu version—half noodles, half salad, all flavor. I eat this when it's hot or when I need something clean and cleansing. Here many of my favorite things jump into the same bowl: crispy tofu, bright and zippy vegetables, grassy avocado, and sprightly herbs.

If you can get your hands on them, some Vietnamese herbs would take this *bun cha* to the next level—Vietnamese basil, mint, cilantro, and pasilla chile—but I've kept it simple with some mint and cilantro here.

........................................................................................

First, chop the tofu into ½-inch/1-cm fingers and put into a bowl. Finely chop the chile, garlic, and the lemongrass stalk, then put half the chile and garlic aside for later and add the rest to the bowl of tofu with all the lemongrass, the soy sauce, and the juice of half the lime. Put the tofu to one side.

Mix the juice from the other lime half with the peanut butter and a splash of water and put to one side.

Next, put the noodles into a bowl, cover with boiling water and leave to soak for 3 minutes, or follow the package instructions.

Now chop the vegetables—you can use a food processor or a mandoline to speed this up. Shred the iceberg and cut the carrot and cucumber into

## SERVES 2

### FOR THE TOFU
7 ounces/200 g firm tofu
1 red chile
1 clove garlic
½ stalk of lemongrass
1 tablespoon soy sauce or tamari
1 lime
1 tablespoon peanut butter
coconut oil

### FOR THE NOODLES AND VEGGIES
4 ounces/125 g rice vermicelli
½ small head of iceberg lettuce
1 large carrot
½ cucumber
2 green onions
½ ripe avocado
a small bunch of cilantro
1¾ ounces/50 g unsalted peanuts
a small bunch of mint or other herbs (see headnote)

### FOR THE DRESSING
2 teaspoons runny honey or maple syrup
1 tablespoon soy sauce or tamari
juice of 2 limes

⋮⋰ CONTINUED

matchsticks. Finely slice the green onions and slice the avocado thinly. Coarsely chop the cilantro and then the peanuts.

Make the dressing by mixing the reserved chile and garlic with the rest of the dressing ingredients.

Heat a pan and add a little coconut oil. Drain the tofu, reserving the marinade. Once the pan is hot, add the tofu to the pan and fry until browned on all sides, then add the peanut butter mixture and the reserved marinade and toss to coat. Take off the heat.

Pile the drained noodles into two bowls and top with the vegetables, cilantro, peanuts, and the mint or herb sprigs. Finally, put the tofu and any of the marinade left in the pan on top and pour over the dressing. Mix at the table.

# goodness bowls

I make a goodness bowl for myself at least once a week; they are a quick, easy, and totally adaptable dinner that can be tweaked throughout the seasons to be hearty, light, refreshing—whatever you feel like. I have laid out the building blocks and given you some examples of my favorites. Check out my recipes for Seeded halloumi and harissa rainbow bowl (page 76) and Plantain, avocado, and black bean bowl (page 68) to get the idea.

Here are some of the ingredients I use most often. Pick from each column. Make a dressing with one part acid (lemon/vinegar) to two parts oil and you can't go wrong.

| HEARTINESS: GRAIN/ BEAN OR LEGUME → | 2 TO 4 SEASONAL VEGGIES → |
|---|---|
| quinoa | shaved raw beets |
| millet | scrunched greens |
| amaranth | sautéed carrots |
| beans | roasted butternut squash |
| pearl barley | roasted sweet potato |
| soba noodles | sautéed potato |
| | pan-fried mushrooms |
| | grated carrot |
| | roasted celery root |
| | tomatoes |
| | roasted cauliflower |
| | steamed broccoli |
| | blanched kale |
| | avocado |

**SOME FAVORITE COMBINATIONS**

| | | | |
|---|---|---|---|
| **1** | quinoa → | kale<br>peas<br>broccoli | → |
| **2** | brown rice → | spinach<br>carrots<br>sugar snap peas | → |
| **3** | lima beans → | greens<br>sweet potatoes<br>tomatoes | → |

| A FLAVOR BOOSTER → | A KILLER DRESSING → | HERBS → | FINISHING TOUCH/ TEXTURE |
|---|---|---|---|
| sautéed onions | miso | parsley | toasted nuts |
| sautéed leeks | harissa | cilantro | toasted seeds |
| jarred roasted red peppers | tahini | fried sage | croutons |
| sautéed green onions | mustard | mint | feta |
| sautéed ginger and garlic | citrus | dill | goat cheese |
| pickled red cabbage | pesto | fried thyme | Manchego |
| sauerkraut | hummus | fried rosemary | Parmesan |
| | yogurt | basil | crumbled crackers |
| | tzatziki | arugula | |
| | mango chutney | | |

. . . . . . . . . . . . . . . . . . . . . . . . . . . . . . . . . . . . . . . . . . . . . . . . . . . . . . . . . . . . . . . . . . . . . . . . . . . . . . . . . . . . . . . . . . . . .

| | → | harissa<br>lemon<br>extra-virgin olive oil | → | mint<br>parsley | → | |
|---|---|---|---|---|---|---|
| sautéed green onions | → | harissa<br>lemon<br>extra-virgin olive oil | → | mint<br>parsley | → | toasted almonds |
| crispy fried onions | → | sesame oil<br>soy sauce<br>rice wine vinegar | → | cilantro | → | toasted sesame seeds |
| roasted red peppers | → | lemon<br>olive oil<br>smoked paprika | → | parsley | → | toasted sourdough, crumbled |

# Plantain, avocado, and black bean bowl

Sometimes I fall head over heels for a food and I can't stop eating it. For a few weeks this year it was plantain. It fills the greengrocers around where I live and I almost always pass my hand over it to reach for sweet potatoes or parsnips. Well, no more. Plantain is my new sweet potato; it adds natural sweetness to my dinners and is super quick to cook and prepare. This dish is my love letter to plantain: I promise I'll never overlook you again.

This bowl is a meeting place for a whole world of flavors: chile-spiked, smoky black beans, caramel-crusted plantain, creamy avocado, sweet leeks, and zingy lime. It's a serious flavor-filled bowl of goodness.

It also works really well with short-grain brown rice in place of the quinoa. I opt for brown rice when I feel like something more filling, but it takes much longer to cook, so bear that in mind.

Fill and boil a kettle of water and get all your ingredients and equipment together.

Measure out the quinoa in a mug or measuring cup, making note of the level it comes up to, then pour it into a large saucepan. Fill the mug to the same level with boiling water and add to the pan, then repeat so you have double the volume of water to quinoa. Add the stock powder or cube, put the pan over high heat, and cook the quinoa at a steady simmer for 10 to 12 minutes, until almost all the water has been absorbed and the little curly grain has been released from each quinoa seed.

Chop the chile. Pour the black beans (including the liquid) into a pan, add half the chopped chile and the cinnamon, and simmer until the beans are thick and almost all the liquid is gone.

CONTINUED

SERVES 4

a mugful of quinoa
(about 7 ounces/200 g)

1 tablespoon vegetable stock powder or ½ stock cube

1 green chile

1 (14-ounce/400-g) can black beans

a pinch of ground cinnamon

2 large leeks

coconut oil

2 handfuls of interesting mushrooms (about 9 ounces/250 g)

2 ripe avocados

2 limes

2 large plantains

Meanwhile, place a pan over high heat. Trim, wash, and finely chop both leeks, add them to the pan with a little coconut oil, sweat for 10 minutes until soft, then transfer them from the pan to a bowl using a slotted spoon. Chop the mushrooms into bite-size pieces. Put the pan back on the heat and add a little more coconut oil and the mushrooms. Pan-fry until crisp, then add to the bowl of leeks.

Mash the avocados with the other half of the chopped chile and the juice of one of the limes.

Put the pan back on the heat. Peel the plantains, cut into ½-inch/ 1-cm-thick slices and add to the pan, allowing each piece to caramelize before turning it over and doing the same on the other side.

Drain the quinoa and divide among four big bowls. Top with the leeks and mushrooms, a few spoonfuls of black beans, and the plantain, and finish with a healthy spoonful of mashed chile avocado and the other lime cut into wedges.

# Sweet potato, lime, and peanut soup

I started making this soup one January when Christmas had been and gone and I was a little jaded by wintry food. I wanted something warming, filling, refreshing, and restoring all at once. It has become the soup that I just can't stop making. It may not sound like much, but the beauty of it is in the few ingredients and the simple, zippy but hearty flavor.

The soup is good on its own, but to really make it sing, I spend the time while it's cooking making a crispy topping, which I toss with lime zest and some peanuts to amp up the flavor.

The clever bit here is using peanut butter to make the soup delicious and creamy. It's a good hit of protein and adds a deep earthiness. It's important to buy a good one, with no added ingredients like palm oil. I make my own and store it in jars that last me a month—it's much fresher and, I am sure, more nourishing, an investment that I use for breakfast and in sauces and soups. (For my nut butter recipes, see page 226.)

SERVES 4

FOR THE SOUP

2 leeks

coconut oil

2 pounds/1 kg sweet potatoes (about 4)

a thumb-size piece of ginger

1 tablespoon vegetable stock powder or ½ stock cube

1 tablespoon soy sauce or tamari

1 tablespoon maple syrup

1 tablespoon peanut butter

sea salt

FOR THE TOPPING

1 shallot

a thumb-size piece of ginger

coconut oil

a handful of unsalted roasted peanuts

2 unwaxed limes

Fill and boil a kettle of water and get all your ingredients and equipment together. Put a large pan over low heat.

Trim and wash the leeks and finely chop them. Add a dollop of coconut oil to the pan and, once it has melted, throw in the leeks. Cook over high heat for 3 to 4 minutes, stirring from time to time, until soft.

While the leeks are cooking, peel the sweet potatoes and chop into rough ½-inch/1-cm dice. Peel and grate the ginger. Once the leeks are cooked, add the sweet potatoes and ginger with 6 cups/1.5 liters of hot water from the kettle and the stock powder, then bring to a boil and simmer for 10 minutes, until the potatoes are cooked. Top up with more hot water if needed.

⋰⋱ CONTINUED

Meanwhile, for the topping, put a frying pan over high heat. Peel and finely slice the shallot and peel and grate the second piece of ginger. Put a dollop of coconut oil into the hot pan, then add the shallot and ginger and fry until really crisp. Drain on paper towels. Coarsely chop the peanuts and put them into a bowl. Grate over the zest of one of the limes.

Once you can mash the sweet potatoes against the side of the pan, the soup is ready. Purée in the pan using a handheld blender until you get a nice smooth consistency. Add the soy sauce, maple syrup, peanut butter, and the juice of the zested lime and blend again to mix. Taste and adjust as needed, adding more lime, soy, and maple until it tastes great; you can add a little sea salt here too, if you like. You are aiming for a deeply flavored soup that balances the sweetness from the potatoes with the earthy peanut butter, and there should be a good back note of ginger and lime too.

Ladle into bowls, top with the crispy shallots and peanuts, and serve with the second lime, cut into wedges, for squeezing over.

# Quick saffron polenta bake

Warming saffron-scented polenta is double-cooked here—first in the pan and then under the broiler with a scattering of tomatoes and feta. The feta crisps and the tomatoes burst as the polenta finishes cooking.

This polenta will be wet, like mashed potatoes or thick rice pudding, not set, which makes it even more satisfying and comforting.

I love the warming sunny flavor of saffron but it can be pricey. If you don't have any at home, you can make this without it, or use another herb like thyme or oregano. It won't taste the same as the saffron but it will add another dimension to your polenta.

........................................................................................................................

Get all your ingredients together and preheat the broiler to high.

Put the polenta, saffron, and olive oil in the bottom of a deep, ovenproof 10-inch/25-cm frying pan over medium heat. Gradually pour in the stock, whisking to prevent lumps. Keep whisking until the mixture thickens and starts to bubble, which will take 5 to 6 minutes. Season well with salt and pepper.

Shred the spinach and coarsely chop the basil, then remove the pan from the heat and stir the spinach and basil into the polenta.

Scatter the tomatoes over the spinach polenta and season well with pepper (no salt if you're using the feta, as it is salty), then crumble over the feta and grate over the zest of the lemon.

Put the pan under the hot broiler for 10 to 12 minutes, until the tomato skins have burst and burnished and the feta has browned and crisped with the heat. Allow to cool for a few minutes before dressing with arugula and pine nuts and serving in the middle of the table for everyone to help themselves.

SERVES 4

1 cup/150 g quick-cooking polenta
a good pinch of saffron strands
3 tablespoons/50 ml olive oil
3 cups/750 ml hot vegetable stock
sea salt and freshly ground pepper
3½ ounces/100 g spinach
a small bunch of basil
9 ounces/250 g cherry tomatoes
3½ ounces/100 g feta cheese (optional)
1 unwaxed lemon
a handful of arugula, to serve
a handful of toasted pine nuts

# Winter root vegetable soba noodles with pickled greens

Soba noodles have become a weekly dinner at my house; they are so quick to cook but don't leave you feeling as if you need a lie-down, like a bowl of pasta or more traditional noodles would. I usually mix them with whatever vegetables I have in the fridge, making something fast, fresh, bright, and pickled to counter the buckwheat's natural sweetness.

Here I use beets and carrots and make a speedy pickle out of some winter greens, but any quick-cooking veggies would do well.

Get all your ingredients together.

Peel the carrot and cut into thin rounds or matchsticks as you like, then do the same with the beet. Put a splash of olive oil into a frying pan, then peel and coarsely chop the ginger, add to the pan, and cook for a minute. Add the carrot and beet, a good pinch of salt, and about 7 tablespoons/ 100 ml of water and cook for 5 to 6 minutes, until all the liquid has evaporated and the carrot and beet have softened.

In the meantime, cook the noodles according to the package instructions, then drain and cool in cold water.

Shred the greens and mix them with the vinegar, a pinch of salt, and 1 teaspoon of the maple syrup. Scrunch them in your hands for a minute to mix the flavors together.

Add the sesame oil, soy, the other teaspoon of maple syrup, the juice of the lime, and the black sesame seeds to the carrot and beet. Throw in the noodles and toss in the dressing.

Serve the noodles in deep bowls, with the pickled greens and chopped cilantro leaves on top, plus some more black sesame seeds and extra limes.

SERVES 2

1 large carrot

1 large beet

olive oil

a thumb-size piece of ginger

sea salt

7 ounces/200 g soba noodles
(I use 100 percent buckwheat ones)

3½ ounces/100 g kale or chard

4 tablespoons brown rice vinegar

2 teaspoons maple syrup

1 teaspoon sesame oil

2 tablespoons soy sauce or tamari

1 lime, plus more for serving

1 tablespoon black sesame seeds,
plus extra to serve

leaves from a small bunch of cilantro

# Seeded halloumi and harissa rainbow bowl

This is a bowl filled with a few favorite things, as well as a killer harissa dressing, burnished seed-encrusted halloumi, my new favorite grain (freekeh), and, of course, some avocado. I vary the veggies I use here according to the season. I have given you my summer version in the recipe, but below are some ideas for the rest of the year.

spring: asparagus, peas, spring greens
summer: tomatoes, yellow beets, kale
autumn: red beets, grated carrot, kale
winter: have a bowl of soup instead

Freekeh is a type of wheat; the word means "rubbed" in Arabic. The story goes that in 2300 BCE, a shed containing the harvest's young green wheat burnt down. The locals thought the crop was ruined, but they discovered that rubbing the burnt husk off the wheat left it edible and in fact toasty and delicious. If you can't get freekeh, any quick-cooking grain like millet or quinoa would work too.

........................................................................

Measure out the freekeh in a mug or measuring cup, making a note of the level it comes up to, then put it into a bowl and cover it with cold water. Rub the grains in your hands, then drain and wash once more in the same way. Put the freekeh into a pan. Fill the mug or jug to the same level with water and add to the pan, then repeat so you have double the volume of water as of freekeh. Add a pinch of salt and a dollop of coconut oil, bring to a boil, and simmer for 15 minutes, until soft but still with a little bite.

Meanwhile, make the dressing. Finely slice the green onions and fry them in a little coconut oil until just starting to brown, then scoop them into a jug and add the honey, harissa, olive oil, and lemon juice. Season with salt and pepper and mix well.

CONTINUED

## SERVES 4

1 cup/150 g freekeh
sea salt
coconut oil
10 ounces/300 g (or a very big handful) cherry tomatoes
4 beets (I use yellow ones)
7 ounces/200 g kale (I use purple)
1 lime
1 ripe avocado
7 ounces/200 g halloumi cheese
2 tablespoons mixed seeds (I use poppy and sesame)
juice of ½ lemon
freshly ground pepper
a small bunch of mint
a small bunch of dill

### FOR THE DRESSING

a bunch of green onions
1 teaspoon runny honey
1 tablespoon harissa
2 tablespoons extra-virgin olive oil
juice of ½ lemon
sea salt and freshly ground pepper

Cut the tomatoes in half. Peel the beets, and use a mandoline or your excellent knife skills to slice them very finely. Remove the stalks and shred the leaves of the kale, put into a bowl with the juice of the lime and a pinch of salt, and scrunch with your hands for a minute.

Cut the avocado in half and remove the pit, then, with the skin still on, use a small knife to make incisions lengthwise along the avocado to form slices.

Put a frying pan over high heat and slice the halloumi thinly. Have your seeds standing by. Put the halloumi into the hot dry pan and cook until brown on one side, which will take about a minute, then flip over and brown the other side. Scatter over the seeds and turn the halloumi in the pan until it is coated with them. Take off the heat.

Once the freekeh is cooked, drain it and dress it with the lemon juice, a drizzle of olive oil, and a pinch each of salt and pepper. Chop the mint and dill and mix into the freekeh.

Serve in shallow bowls, topped with all the rainbow vegetables, the seeded halloumi, and generous spoonfuls of the harissa dressing.

# Green mimosa salad

My first real job as a chef was at a beautiful local old-world restaurant in Kensington called Daphne's. It was supposed to be Princess Diana's favorite—you get the vibe: starched tablecloths, Chablis, and charming waiters who had been there so long they had become part of the furniture. It was perfectly calm and pretty posh, with clean, simple salads and pastas.

I worked the starters and pastry sections both at once, quite a baptism of fire. One of the things I remember most was a dressing they made, a mimosa dressing of good Chardonnay vinegar, oil, and herbs. Through a hot summer, I must have dressed a thousand salads with it. In summer, I often crave the simplicity of it on some greens.

I've made this more of a meal, though, by adding eggs. The eggs are mimosa eggs—I've shredded them, which may sound a bit funny at first, but it's super quick and keeps things really light and clean. If you are vegan, you can boil and grate in a few potatoes in place of the eggs—it's still delicious.

SERVES 4

6 free-range or organic eggs

17 ounces/500 g asparagus

7 ounces/200 g broccolini stems

sea salt

½ shallot

2 tablespoons good Chardonnay vinegar (white wine vinegar will do in a pinch)

1 tablespoon extra-virgin olive oil

1 tablespoon Dijon mustard

freshly ground pepper

1 ripe avocado

a good bunch of dill or fennel tops

1 unwaxed lemon

Greek yogurt or crème fraîche (optional)

TO SERVE (OPTIONAL)

good rye bread (see page 254)

butter

Fill and boil a kettle of water and get all your ingredients together.

Put the eggs into a small saucepan and cover them with boiling water from the kettle. Put over medium heat and bring back to a boil, then simmer for 7 minutes.

Next, snap the tough ends off the asparagus and discard them (you can use them for stock, if you like). Chop the asparagus stems into ½-inch/ 1-cm rounds, stopping when you get near the top and keeping the tips intact. Chop the broccolini in the same way, stopping when you get close to the floret.

⋰· CONTINUED

Put the asparagus tips and broccolini florets into a larger saucepan and cover with boiling water. Add a good pinch of salt and simmer for 3 minutes, then add the asparagus and broccolini rounds for a final minute.

Chop the shallot finely and put it into a large mixing bowl. Add the vinegar, oil, mustard, and a good pinch each of salt and pepper and stir to combine.

Once the green vegetables have had their cooking time, drain in a colander and add them to the bowl. While the veggies are still warm, toss in the dressing. Pit the avocado and cut it into thick slices. Scoop out and add this to the bowl.

Once the eggs are cooked, drain them too and run them under cold water until they are cool enough to handle. Coarsely chop the dill or fennel tops. Once the eggs are cool, peel them and grate them into a bowl. Season with salt and pepper, grate over the zest of the lemon, scatter over the dill or fennel, and mix gently. If you like, you can add a tablespoon of crème fraîche or Greek yogurt here.

Serve the veggies with spoonfuls of the lemon-and-dill shredded eggs, and a little buttered rye bread if you like.

# Cashew, kale, and lime nacho bowl

Every time I order nachos at a restaurant, I am disappointed. They always seem to consist of a pile of oversalted tortilla chips, mountains of rubbery cheese, an afterthought salsa, and a scoop of guacamole.

I think nachos deserve more than that, as the layering of flavors and textures in a bowl of nachos has so much potential. Here, homemade tortilla chips are topped with crispy lime-spiked kale, a punchy green chile–cashew cream, and fresh pops of corn and cilantro. There is a little cheese, but if that's not your thing, you can skip it, as the nachos will still be flavor-packed.

Here I am not going to recommend using the pure corn tortillas that I usually seek out in Mexican cooking, as they will dry out in the oven; good whole-grain or gluten-free tortillas work well, as do soft corn tortillas, but be sure to check the back of the package, as a lot of brands contain unnecessary extras. If you don't recognize what's in them, look elsewhere.

..................................................................................

Preheat the oven to 425°F/220°C (convection 400°F/200°C). Fill and boil a kettle of water and get all your ingredients together. Put the cashews into a bowl, cover with boiling water, and set aside.

Put your tortillas in a stack and cut them first in half across the middle, then into quarters, and then into eighths, so you have tortilla-chip-shaped pieces. Put them into the largest baking dish you have, making sure they don't overlap too much, then drizzle them with a little oil and sprinkle with salt, pepper, and some smoked paprika.

Stem the kale and rip into pieces. Put on another large baking dish, grate over the zest of 1 lime, drizzle over a little oil, and sprinkle with salt and pepper.

⋮· CONTINUED

**SERVES 4 AS A MEAL OR 6 AS A SNACK**

3½ ounces/100 g raw unsalted cashews

6 soft whole-wheat tortillas (see headnote)

olive or canola oil

sea salt and freshly ground pepper

½ teaspoon smoked paprika

7 ounces/200 g kale

2 unwaxed limes, plus extra for serving

2 green chiles

a bunch of cilantro

2 ears corn

1 ripe avocado

3½ ounces/100 g good cheddar or Manchego cheese

Put both dishes into the oven for 10 to 15 minutes, until the kale is crisp and the tortillas are nicely browned.

While that is happening, make the cashew cream. You really need a decent blender here, though a handheld blender and a deep jar will do. Drain the cashews and put them into the blender with the juice of the zested lime and a good pinch of salt. Coarsely chop the green chiles and add to the blender (taking the seeds out if you don't like things super fiery), and add the stalks from the bunch of cilantro too.

Pour in ½ cup/130 ml of water and blend on high for a couple of minutes, until you have a smooth, grassy-green cream. Taste and add more salt, lime, and chile as needed until it tastes great. If it's looking a bit thick, add another tablespoon of water.

Cut the kernels from the ears of corn with a sharp knife—I rest the cobs in a mixing bowl while I do this so the kernels don't go everywhere. Pit and slice the avocado and squeeze over half of the remaining lime.

Once the tortillas and kale are ready, take them out of the oven and turn the broiler on to high. Scatter the kale over the tortillas and grate over the cheese. Put everything under the broiler to brown for a couple of minutes, until the cheese is beginning to bubble.

Spoon on the cashew cream, scoop out the avocado, and scatter over the corn and cilantro leaves. Serve with extra lime wedges for squeezing.

# Sesame, pistachio, and preserved lemon crispy rice

There is something so satisfying about a simple, well-flavored pilaf—a pan full of gently but generously spiced rice for dinner. Here I cook the rice for a little longer than you might expect to get a crispy crust on the bottom; this is called *tadig* in Farsi and, to my mind, it is the holy grail of rice. If you are in a hurry, then you can skip this stage. If you don't have preserved lemons, then the zest of a couple of lemons would work well in their place.

Fill and boil a kettle of water and get all your ingredients together.

Rinse your rice under cold running water for a minute or so, then put it into a measuring cup and make a note of where it comes up to. Put a pan over medium heat and add a dollop of coconut oil. Once the oil is hot, add the rice and fry in the coconut oil for a couple of minutes. Next, fill the measuring cup with the same volume of hot water from the kettle as the rice and add to the pan, then repeat so you have double the amount of water as rice in the pan. Add the saffron and bashed cardamom pods to the pan as well. Put the lid on and cook for 15 minutes, until the rice has absorbed all the water and is fluffy.

While the rice is cooking, toast the sesame seeds and pistachios in a dry frying pan until just browned and fragrant. Halve the preserved lemons, scoop out the middles and discard, then finely chop the rind. Remove the seeds from the pomegranate. I do this by cutting it in half and holding one half, cut-side down, in my hand over a bowl and tapping it with a wooden spoon so that the seeds fall out. Chop the parsley and dill leaves. Mix the yogurt with the zest and juice of the lemon and the herbs and season well.

Once the rice is ready, make three holes in it and add a little more coconut oil to each. Put over high heat for 8 minutes so that the rice crisps up at the bottom. Once it's crispy, take off the heat and spoon onto a platter. Mix with the nuts, seeds, preserved lemon, and pomegranate seeds. Serve generous bowls of the rice topped with the herbed yogurt and some arugula or watercress.

## SERVES 4

¾ cup/150 g brown basmati rice

coconut oil

a good pinch of saffron

6 cardamom pods, bashed

4 tablespoons sesame seeds

1¾ ounces/50 g pistachios

4 preserved lemons

1 pomegranate

leaves from a small bunch of parsley

leaves from a small bunch of dill

½ cup/100 ml yogurt

1 unwaxed lemon

a couple of handfuls of arugula or watercress

# Black-eyed peas with chard and green herb smash

This is a super-quick stew which has its roots in Palestine. Pick your chard color here—the clean green Swiss or the sweet-shop-neon rainbow chard. It is not often that one vegetable provides such a bouquet of options.

Black-eyed peas were often overlooked in my kitchen in favor of buttery cannellini, earthy black beans, or plump lima beans. No longer though; black-eyed peas are a new favorite. Sometimes, I like to top this with tahini for an extra layer of flavor.

....................................................................................................

Fill and boil a kettle of water and get all your ingredients together. Put a large saucepan over heat.

Wash and finely slice the leek. Add to the saucepan with the coconut or olive oil and cook over medium heat for a couple of minutes, until soft and sweet. Finely slice the garlic and add to the pan with the chile powder and cook for a couple of minutes, until the garlic is beginning to brown. Add the passata and black-eyed peas with their liquid, the stock powder, and ⅔ cup/200 ml of hot water from the kettle and bring to a simmer. Grate in the nutmeg, squeeze in the juice of the half lemon, add the squeezed lemon half to the pan, and simmer for 10 minutes or so. Meanwhile, strip the leaves from the chard stalks. Finely slice the stalks and add them to the pan, then finely shred the leaves and put to one side.

Put all the ingredients for the herb smash into a food processor and puree until you have a smooth, grassy paste. Season well with salt and pepper.

Once the peas are soft and flavorful and the liquid has reduced to a thick, soup-like consistency, stir in the chard leaves, season well with salt and pepper, and leave to cook for a couple of minutes. Scoop into deep bowls and spoon the herb smash on top. If you're really hungry, some rice or flatbread would go well alongside.

SERVES 4

FOR THE PEAS

1 leek

1 tablespoon coconut oil or olive oil

2 cloves garlic

a good pinch of chile powder or chopped dried chile

1½ cups (400 ml) passata (tomato puree, see page 117)

2 (14-ounce/400-g) cans of black-eyed peas

1 teaspoon vegetable stock powder or ½ stock cube

a good grating of nutmeg

½ unwaxed lemon

7 ounces/200 g bunch of Swiss or rainbow chard

sea salt and freshly ground pepper

FOR THE HERB SMASH

a large bunch of cilantro

2 green chiles

2 cloves garlic

1 ounce/30 g shelled walnuts

1 tablespoon runny honey or maple syrup

2 tablespoons good olive oil

juice of ½ lemon

sea salt and freshly ground pepper

rice or flatbreads, to serve (optional)

# Crispy cauliflower rice with sticky spiced cashews

There is something so subtle and even-tempered about cauliflower. I love to eat it two ways: to highlight its gentleness with subtle bay and cheeses, or to go to the other extreme and hit it with punchy spices and serious flavor—cauliflower holds on to flavor so well.

Here, I make rice out of the cauliflower, which has become quite a thing among healthy eaters. It's often eaten raw, which I have to say isn't for me. Instead I sauté it so it's browned and crispy-edged, and spike it with my favorite southern Indian duo: mustard seeds and curry leaves. It's topped with some freshness from radishes and a crunch from spiced cashews: a dish that sits firmly at the crossroads of healthy and delicious.

If you can't find curry leaves, just leave them out, as I have yet to find an alternative flavor match. I have also made this using broccoli, which is equally delicious.

I suggest using coconut nectar here to sweeten. Coconut nectar is the nutrient-rich sap of the coconut tree. It's harvested by tapping into the tree to release the sap, much like maple syrup. It's packed with nutrients and amino acids and is low GI, so it won't spike your blood sugar like white sugar. I use it anywhere I need a bit of sweetness.

....................................................................................

Get all your ingredients together and set up your food processor.

Take the leaves and gnarly root off your cauliflower and chop it into big chunks. Put them into the food processor and pulse until you have a rice-like texture.

Put your largest frying pan over high heat (if you don't have a nice big one, two smaller ones will work). Finely slice the onion and add to the pan with a good dollop of coconut oil. Cook for 5 minutes, until soft, stirring from time to time. Meanwhile, coarsely chop the garlic and peel and chop

## SERVES 4

1 medium cauliflower
(about 1⅓ pounds/600 g)

1 red onion

coconut oil

2 cloves garlic

a thumb-size piece of ginger

1 tablespoon black mustard seeds

a large handful of fresh curry leaves

sea salt

3½ ounces/100 g cashews

a small bunch of radishes

a small bunch of cilantro

a couple of handfuls of pea shoots
or dainty salad leaves

a squeeze of coconut nectar or honey

a pinch of garam masala

zest and juice of 1 unwaxed lime

### TO SERVE (OPTIONAL)

4 chapatis or rotis

lime pickle or mango chutney

the ginger. Once the onion is soft, add the garlic and ginger, the mustard seeds and curry leaves, and cook for a couple of minutes, then season well with sea salt.

Now turn the heat right up. Add the cauliflower rice and cook, stirring every couple of minutes to make sure all the rice gets a little browned on the bottom of the pan—this will take about 10 minutes.

Meanwhile, in another dry frying pan, toast the cashews until just brown. Thinly slice the radishes, pick the cilantro leaves from their stalks, and mix both with the pea shoots or salad leaves.

When the cashews are toasted, toss them with a little coconut nectar or honey and a pinch of garam masala and take off the heat.

As soon as the cauliflower rice is nicely browned all over, spoon it onto a platter. Crumble over the cashews, scatter over the salad, grate over the zest of the lime, and squeeze over the juice. If you are really hungry, you could serve it with some chapatis or rotis and a little lime pickle or mango chutney.

# Zucchini noodles with pistachio, green herbs, and ricotta

I hesitated to include a recipe for these vegetable noodles, as they are on every scene-y or healthy menu and are peppered through raw and healthy cookbooks. But the fact is they are quick and simple and I love eating them. I am not going to insist that you go out and buy a Spiralizer if you don't have one; I do have one but still often use a Y peeler and a knife rather than getting out this gadget. A julienne peeler, which costs much less, will do exactly the same job and take up much less cupboard space.

Vegans, leave out the ricotta—or you can bake silken tofu in the same way, if you like.

Preheat the oven to 400°F/200°C (convection 375°F/180°C). Fill and boil a kettle of water and get all your ingredients together.

Turn the ricotta out of its package onto a baking dish, grate over the zest of one lemon, sprinkle over a large pinch of dried chile, and drizzle over the honey. Put the ricotta into the oven to bake for 15 minutes, until caramelized on top.

Put the pistachios into the oven to toast for 3 to 5 minutes. Heat a frying pan over high heat and thinly slice one of the unzested lemons, picking out and discarding any seeds. Add a tablespoon of olive oil to the pan and fry the lemon slices until they are burnished and sticky.

Take the pistachios out of the oven and pour into the bowl of your food processor; pick the mint and basil leaves and throw them in too. Add the juice of half the zested lemon and a good pinch of salt. Add 4 tablespoons of olive oil and a tablespoon of cold water, pulse until you have a textured grassy green pesto, then transfer to a bowl.

CONTINUED

SERVES 4

9 ounces/250 g ricotta cheese

3 unwaxed lemons

a good pinch of dried chile flakes

1 teaspoon runny honey

3 ounces/60 g shelled pistachios

extra-virgin olive oil

a small bunch of mint

a small bunch of basil

sea salt

4 large or 6 small zucchini

Now for the zucchini. Use a julienne peeler, or a Spiralizer if you have one, to make zucchini noodles. To do this by hand, use a Y peeler or a mandoline to peel the zucchini into long wide strips. Carefully stack the slices on top of each other and use a knife to cut them into thin strips. This is actually really easy and quick, so don't be put off. Place in a heatproof mixing bowl, cover with boiling water from the kettle, and leave to sit for 2 to 3 minutes.

Once the fried lemon slices are cool enough to handle, coarsely chop them and stir them through the pesto. Remove the ricotta from the oven.

Drain the zucchini noodles well and toss with the pesto. Crumble the ricotta on top and finish with more lemon zest and a drizzle of oil, if you like.

# Charred broccolini with cucumber noodles and peanut sauce

This bowl of freshness and flavor is half based on a bang-up bowl of *dan dan* noodles I ate in L.A. and half based on a charred cauliflower I made a couple of weeks later. I wanted to put the charred smokiness and the peanutty sweetness in one bowl.

Instead of using normal noodles here, I've made some quick cucumber noodles with a Y peeler—they add an amazing freshness and work brilliantly as a foil to the charred smoky broccolini and richly fragrant peanut sauce. If I am really hungry, I serve this with a pile of jasmine rice or noodles.

When you're buying peanut butter, be sure to check the ingredients list— it should have nothing apart from peanuts and perhaps a little salt. If it has anything else, put it back. I use crunchy here, but smooth would work too; I'll leave that up to your own peanut butter leanings. See page 226 for my nut butter recipes.

When you are making the cucumber noodles, you'll be left with the middle of the cucumbers. I usually chop them up and use them to infuse my drinking water in the fridge, but sometimes I purée the middle bits and freeze them in ice cube trays for a cucumber-iced gin and tonic. Seriously good.

.......................................................................................................

Fill and boil a kettle of water and get all your ingredients together.

Trim the broccolini and make an incision down each stalk to help them cook quicker. If you are using normal broccoli, cut the bottom of the stem off and slice into long thin trees. Put the trimmed broccolini into a bowl and cover with boiling water from the kettle. Leave for 5 minutes, then drain and set aside.

CONTINUED

## SERVES 4

### FOR THE BROCCOLI
14 ounces/400 g broccolini, or 1 large head of normal broccoli

coconut oil

3 cloves garlic

3 cucumbers

1 tablespoon runny honey

1 tablespoon tamari or light soy sauce

1 red chile

1 tablespoon sesame oil

1 unwaxed lime

### FOR THE PEANUT GINGER SAUCE
6 tablespoons good peanut butter

a thumb-size piece of ginger

2 tablespoons rice wine vinegar

zest and juice of 1 unwaxed lime

1 tablespoon tamari or soy sauce

1 tablespoon maple syrup

Meanwhile, get a small pan over medium-high heat and add a dollop of coconut oil. Finely slice the garlic and, once the oil is hot, add to the pan. Fry for a couple of minutes until just crisp, being careful not to burn, then drain on kitchen paper.

Next, get on with the cucumber noodles. Use a Y peeler to peel each side of the cucumber into thin ribbons, stopping when you get to the watery middle bit, which doesn't make good noodles, and discarding the peel if you like. (See the headnote for suggestions about what to do with the leftover middles.) Put a griddle over high heat.

Now for the peanut sauce. Whisk the peanut butter with a scant ½ cup/100 ml of warm water, then peel and grate in the ginger, add all the other sauce ingredients, and mix well. Add a little water if needed: you are after heavy-cream consistency.

Toss the broccolini with the honey and soy. Chop the red chile and add to the broccolini along with the sesame oil. Place on the griddle and cook for a couple of minutes on each side, until nicely charred.

Divide the cucumber noodles among four bowls and top with the peanut sauce, broccolini, and crispy garlic. Finish with the zest of the lime, then cut the lime into wedges and serve on the side.

# Quinoa risotto with mashed peas and greens

I feel a bit bad calling this a risotto, really. I spent a good year in the kitchen of Jamie Oliver's London restaurant Fifteen mastering a perfect risotto surrounded by brilliant Italian cooks: the stirring, the creaminess, the perfect rice, the resting, the butter, and the Parmesan. But the reality is, I don't want risotto every day. This is more my style on a weeknight—it's got the warming, hearty, nurturing feeling that I love in a risotto, topped with the freshness of a quick sweet-pea smash, greens, and lots of heady fresh herbs.

In winter I make this with mashed roast carrots or beets in place of the peas and some flash-fried winter greens; the fresh green herbs are replaced with thyme and rosemary oil. Equally delicious.

....................................................................................................

Fill and boil a kettle of water and get all your ingredients together.

Wash and finely slice the leeks. Place a pan over medium-high heat and add a couple of tablespoons of olive oil. Add the leeks and cook until beginning to brown, then finely slice the garlic, add to the pan, and cook for a minute or two.

Meanwhile, add the quinoa and cook for a few minutes, allowing it to pop and crackle and toast; this will give it a much better flavor. Once you've had a few minutes of crackling, add the white wine and the juice of half the lemon and cook until the wine has evaporated. Add the stock powder and 2½ cups/600 ml of boiling water and bring to a gentle simmer.

Measure out the peas into a measuring cup and cover with boiling water from the kettle to defrost them. Shred the greens finely and put to one side. Toast the pine nuts in a dry pan until just browned.

## SERVES 4

2 leeks

olive oil

2 cloves garlic

1½ cups/250 g quinoa

⅞ cup/200 ml white wine

1 lemon

1 tablespoon vegetable stock powder or ½ stock cube

9 ounces/250 g frozen peas

7 ounces/200 g baby kale or spinach

1¾ ounces/50 g pine nuts

a few sprigs of mint

½ a bunch of basil

sea salt

2 ounces/60 g Parmesan cheese (I use a vegetarian one), plus more to serve

freshly ground pepper

3½ ounces/100 g ricotta or feta cheese (optional)

Drain the defrosted peas and put into the jar of a blender. Pick the mint and basil leaves from the stalks and add to the blender with a good pinch of salt, the juice of the other half lemon, and 1 tablespoon of olive oil and blend until smooth.

When the quinoa is the consistency of loose porridge, cover and keep over low heat. Stir the shredded greens into the quinoa, adding a little more boiling water if you need to, to get it to a loose risotto consistency. Grate in the Parmesan and stir. Season well with pepper—you won't need much salt, as the stock will be salty.

Serve the quinoa topped with the pea mash, toasted pine nuts, the crumbled ricotta or feta, if using, and a final grating of Parmesan.

# Beet and buckwheat pancakes

This is a brilliantly vibrant dinner of reds, greens, oranges, and golden browns, and it looks so pretty on the plate. Buckwheat and beet make these pancakes more satisfying and hearty than normal ones. If you can't get buckwheat flour, spelt or whole wheat will do in its place. You can make the pancakes with carrots instead of beets, in which case they are best topped with almonds and lime zest.

Get all your ingredients and equipment together.

Put the buckwheat flour and baking powder into a bowl and whisk in 1 cup/ 250 ml of the milk and then the egg (if you are using chia seeds, add those instead of the egg, along with 3 tablespoons of cold water). Add a pinch of salt and grate in the beet using a fine grater. Leave the batter to sit while you get on with a few other things. It will thicken while it sits. You're after a thick pancake-batter consistency. You can add a little more milk if you need to.

Heat a pan over high heat, add the hazelnuts, and toast until golden brown. Put to one side. Pit the olives. Put the pan back on the heat and add a teaspoon of coconut oil, then the olives. Fry until they are beginning to crisp, then take them out of the pan and put aside for later.

Now back to the pancakes. Put the pan back on the heat and add a little more coconut oil. Once the oil is hot, add 2 tablespoons of the batter to make little pancakes, fitting as many into the pan as you can. Cook for 2 to 3 minutes, until bubbles appear on the top and they are starting to crisp up around the sides, then flip and cook on the other side for 1 to 2 minutes. Keep warm while you make the rest. If you are in a hurry, you can have two pans going at once.

Once the pancakes are all cooked, pile them onto four plates and top them with a little goat cheese, the toasted hazelnuts, a pile of greens, the crisped olives, and a grating of orange zest.

SERVES 4
(MAKES 12 PANCAKES)

1½ cups/250 g buckwheat flour

1 heaping teaspoon baking powder

1 to 1¼ cups/250 to 300 ml unsweetened almond milk or cow's milk

1 free-range or organic egg, or 1 tablespoon chia seeds

sea salt

1 medium beet, peeled

1¾ ounces/50 g blanched hazelnuts

3½ ounces/100 g black olives

coconut oil

4 ounces/125 g soft goat cheese

4 small handfuls of green salad leaves

1 unwaxed orange

# quick 20-minute stir-fries

Follow this formula each time: main veggie, backup veggies, protein, aromatics, rice/noodles, seasoning/dressing, crunch.

You'll need a good wok or frying pan, and to have all your ingredients chopped before you start. Make sure you get your wok or pan screaming hot. Always start by adding the vegetables that will take the longest to cook. Fry for a couple of minutes, turning all the time, then add the remaining vegetables and the protein. Cook until just beginning to brown, then add the aromatics (if you add them at the beginning they'll burn), your cooked rice or noodles, and, finally, any dressing. Add the crunch once the stir-fry is scooped into bowls.

| MAIN VEGGIE → | BACKUP VEGGIES → | PROTEIN → |
|---|---|---|
| BROCCOLI | GREENS | TOFU |
| SWEET POTATO | BROCCOLI<br>BOK CHOY | TEMPEH |
| SQUASH | SUGAR SNAP PEAS<br>SPINACH | SEITAN |
| CABBAGE | CARROTS | PANEER |
| GREENS | GREEN ONIONS<br>BEAN SPROUTS | EGG<br>(BEATEN) |
| MUSHROOMS | SNOW PEAS<br>GREENS | TOFU |

| AROMATICS | → | RICE/ NOODLES | → | SEASONING/ DRESSING | → | CRUNCH |
|---|---|---|---|---|---|---|
| GINGER CHILE GARLIC | | JASMINE RICE | | SESAME OIL SOY SAUCE | | SESAME SEEDS |
| GINGER GARLIC | | SOBA NOODLES | | MISO LIME MAPLE SYRUP | | BLACK SESAME SEEDS |
| GINGER GARLIC GREEN ONIONS | | BROWN RICE | | SESAME OIL RICE WINE MAPLE SYRUP | | CASHEWS |
| GINGER CHILE GARLIC | | BASMATI RICE | | MUSTARD SEEDS HONEY | | TOASTED SLICED ALMONDS |
| GINGER CHILE GARLIC | | FLAT RICE NOODLES | | SOY SAUCE SESAME OIL CHILE SAUCE | | ROASTED PEANUTS |
| GINGER CHILE | | EGG NOODLES | | LIME | | |

A lot can happen in half an hour. This is still quick cooking, but with an opportunity to layer flavor with more subtlety: quinoa cakes, chickpea pancakes, butternut hash, black bean fritters, greens-stuffed burritos, sweet roast zucchini ratatouille, killer chili, speedy spelt pizza, deep and craveworthy chowder, and sticky-sweet chile paneer.

carrot and chickpea pancake with lemon-spiked dressing · squash, greens, and quinoa fritters with sumac yogurt · bloody mary salad with black rice · black bean and corn fritters · butternut and sweet leek hash · 30-minute sweet potato chili · persian pea and herb bakes with beet labneh · squash, roasted tomato, and popped black bean salad · 10 favorite suppers from 10 favorite vegetables · pan-roasted lime, feta, and chile greens burrito · grilled avocado barley bowl · sweet roasted zucchini with crispy chickpeas · 10 simple baked potatoes · charred mushroom and cashew pizza · smoky corn chowder with maple-toasted coconut · green bean and chile paneer · rye pancakes with crispy sunchokes · winter chopped salad with candied seeds

# Carrot and chickpea pancake with lemon-spiked dressing

This is a light but hearty pancake made from chickpea flour and grated carrots. I made these a lot while staying with my sister in California, and they are what Californian cooking is all about for me—delicious, nourishing, light, and bright. Chickpea flour is cheap and easy to find; it will be in the flour or Indian section at the supermarket and may be called gram flour.

The batter can be easily doubled or tripled for more pancakes. It keeps well in the fridge until the next day, if necessary, though you may need to loosen it to pancake-batter consistency with a little more water or milk. For a vegan version, make the sauce using blended soaked cashews in place of the cottage cheese.

First, make your batter. Sift the chickpea flour into a large bowl and add a generous pinch each of salt and pepper. Whisk in the milk and olive oil and let the mixture sit, covered, while you make your sauce.

Finely chop the cornichons and the green chile. Chop the leaves of the parsley and dill. Put all this into a small bowl with the cottage cheese, Worcestershire sauce, chile sauce, and lemon zest. Mix well and season with salt and pepper to taste.

Peel and grate the carrots and stir them into the batter. Place a large nonstick frying pan over high heat and add a teaspoon of ghee or coconut oil. Add the batter and allow it to cook for 4 to 5 minutes, until the pancake is set around the edges and starting to brown and crisp. Place a plate on top of the pancake, then cover your hand with a tea towel and flip the pancake onto the plate. Slide off the plate back into the pan and cook on the other side for 4 to 5 minutes.

Cut the pancake into slices and top with sprouted seeds, salad leaves, and spoonfuls of the sauce.

SERVES 2

FOR THE PANCAKE

1¼ cups/150 g chickpea flour

sea salt and freshly ground pepper

1 cup/230 ml milk of your choice
(I use unsweetened almond)

2 tablespoons extra-virgin olive oil

2 medium carrots

ghee or coconut oil

FOR THE SAUCE

8 cornichons

1 green chile

leaves from a few sprigs of parsley

leaves from a few sprigs of dill

4 tablespoons cottage cheese
or Greek yogurt

½ tablespoon vegetarian
Worcestershire sauce

a splash of chile sauce

zest of ½ unwaxed lemon

sea salt and freshly ground pepper

TO SERVE

a couple of handfuls of sprouted
seeds and legumes

a few handfuls of baby salad leaves

# Squash, greens, and quinoa fritters with sumac yogurt

These fritters are hearty without leaving you feeling groaningly full.

Don't be tempted to skip the lemon and sumac yogurt, as it really makes these little cakes sing. I like to use a mixture of different-colored quinoa here, as it adds to the beauty of the green and sunset orange–flecked fritters. The mixture keeps well in the fridge if you want to cook the fritters as you go, and the cooked fritters keep for a couple of days in the fridge—they are great torn and tucked into a flatbread with some leaves for lunch, or in a good bun instead of a burger.

To make this vegan, use silken tofu in place of the feta and 4 tablespoons of chia seeds soaked to a gel in 12 tablespoons of water to replace the eggs, and be more generous with the seasoning.

....................................................................................................................

Fill and boil a kettle of water and get all your ingredients and equipment together.

If you are cooking the quinoa, weigh it out into a mug, noting the level it comes up to, quickly rinse under cold water, then pour it into a pan. Fill the mug to the same level with water and add to the pan, then repeat so you have double the volume of water as quinoa. Bring to a boil, then turn down the heat and simmer for 10 to 12 minutes, until almost all the water has been absorbed and the little curly grain has been released from each quinoa seed.

Meanwhile, peel, seed, and grate the squash and add it to the quinoa (the squash doesn't need to be submerged; it can steam on top of the quinoa). Simmer for the last 2 to 3 minutes of the quinoa's cooking time, until it has lost its rawness and is mushy. Drain, if there is any water

⋮ CONTINUED

## SERVES 4 (MAKES 8 FRITTERS)

a mugful of uncooked red, white, or black quinoa (about 5 ounces/150 g), or 2 mugfuls of cooked quinoa (about 10 ounces/300 g)

a 14-ounce/400-g piece of butternut squash

a bunch of green onions

7 ounces/200 g fresh greens (spinach, kale, or chard)

⅔ cup/60 g rolled oats

1 teaspoon toasted cumin seeds

7 ounces/200 g feta cheese

sea salt and freshly ground pepper

1 unwaxed lemon

4 free-range or organic eggs

a small bunch of parsley

a small bunch of cilantro

extra-virgin olive oil

## FOR THE YOGURT

⅔ cup/150 ml yogurt of your choice (I use Greek or coconut)

sea salt

1 teaspoon sumac or dried chile

## TO SERVE

½ English cucumber

4 ripe tomatoes

a handful of good black olives

4 handfuls of salad leaves

remaining, then put back on the heat and cook for a couple of minutes
to get rid of all the moisture—you should hear a crackle. Spread out on
a baking sheet to cool quickly.

Finely chop the green onions and shred the greens. Place in a large mixing
bowl with the oats and cumin. Crumble in the feta, then add some salt
and pepper and the zest of the lemon and mix well. Add the cooled
quinoa (it can still be slightly warm) and the eggs, then coarsely chop and
stir in the herbs. Mix well and put into the fridge while you get on with
another couple of jobs.

Use this time to get your salad ready: peel, seed, and slice the cucumber,
slice the tomatoes, and pit the olives. Mix the lot with the juice of half the
zested lemon and a drizzle of olive oil and season with salt and pepper.
Divide the leaves among four bowls and top with the tomato mixture.

Mix the yogurt with some salt and the juice of the other half of the lemon,
then stir in the sumac or chile.

Take the quinoa mixture out of the fridge and mold into eight rough
patties with your hands. Heat a light coating of oil in a frying pan over
medium heat. Add the patties and fry for about 4 minutes on each side,
until golden brown.

Serve the fritters with generous spoonfuls of the yogurt and salad.

# Bloody Mary salad with black rice

Black rice is also, magically, known as forbidden rice. It's dense and craveworthy, and cooked this way it has a comforting starchiness that is offset by the Bloody Mary–dressed tomatoes and some quick-pickled onions. If you have lovage growing in your garden or see it in your local shop, it would be a brilliant addition here, but for most people it's hard to find, so I've left it out.

Black rice is cultivated in Asia, and it is my new favorite. It's usually unmilled, with the fiber-rich black husks still intact. It is this outer layer that sets black rice apart from other types of unmilled rice, as the deep, dark pigments it contains boast special nutrients, the same ones you find in antioxidant-rich black grapes and blueberries. As it is unmilled, it takes longer to cook than white rice.

In the winter I eat this black rice with roasted beets in place of the tomatoes. The colors are amazing—deep hues of winter.

If you have time, soak the rice overnight in double the volume of cold water; if not, don't sweat, it will just take a little longer to cook. By celery heart, I mean just the center few stalks of the celery, the point at which they turn more yellow than green. If you are using jarred horseradish, try to search out the pure grated stuff, which is stronger and hasn't been mixed into a horseradish sauce or cream. I serve this with a simple arugula or watercress salad.

.............................................................................................

Get all your ingredients together and boil a kettle of water.

Rinse the rice under cold running water. Place it in a saucepan with 1 quart/ 1 liter of hot water, cover with a lid, bring to a boil, then lower the heat and

⠿ CONTINUED

## SERVES 4

1¼ cups/250 g black rice

1 small red onion

3 tablespoons sherry
or red wine vinegar

sea salt

17 ounces/500 g different-colored
tomatoes

1 celery heart

3½ ounces/100 g fat black olives

## FOR THE DRESSING

2 tablespoons extra-virgin olive oil

1 tablespoon vegetarian
Worcestershire sauce

1 teaspoon Tabasco or similar
chile sauce

freshly ground pepper

2 tablespoons freshly grated
or jarred horseradish

1 lemon

cook gently for about 30 minutes (or up to 50 minutes if it is unsoaked), or until the rice is tender and all the water has been absorbed.

Finely slice the red onion, then put it into a bowl with a tablespoon of the vinegar and a good pinch of salt and give it all a good scrunch to help it pickle.

Chop the tomatoes into shapes and sizes that make the most of their own individual beauty. Very finely slice the celery (keeping the inner leaves for later), pit and coarsely chop the olives, and put everything into a big bowl.

Now make your dressing. Mix the oil and the remaining 2 tablespoons of vinegar in a little bowl, then add the Worcestershire sauce and Tabasco; pour over the tomato mixture. Season the lot with some more salt and pepper, grate or scatter over the horseradish, toss together, and leave to one side for the flavors to develop.

Once the rice is cooked, drain any excess water (there may not be any if you measured spot on) and season with salt and pepper. Squeeze over the juice of the lemon. The rice will be thick and sticky, a bit like black rice pudding, but should loosen a little once the lemon juice has been stirred in. Spoon the rice onto a platter, top with the onions, then the tomatoes, and, finally, scatter over the celery leaves.

# Black bean and corn fritters

These cumin-spiked fritters are super quick and easy. They are made with ingredients I almost always have on hand and, in a fix, canned corn would work too.

The avocado smash I make to go with these fritters is spiked with three types of citrus, which makes it super refreshing. I chop the citrus whole, which works so well; just take care to cut away any pith, and make sure you cut out the pithy part in the middle too. If you are in a hurry, just use the zest and a little juice instead. I like to serve this with a lime-dressed green salad. These fritters are also great torn up like falafel in flatbreads with crunchy lettuce and hummus.

......................................................................................................................

**SERVES 4
(MAKES 8 FRITTERS)**

7 ounces/200 g spinach
or other greens

1 (14-ounce/400-g) can
of black beans

2 ears corn

1 red chile

a small bunch of cilantro

4 free-range or organic eggs

sea salt and freshly ground pepper

a good pinch of cumin seeds

coconut oil

**FOR THE AVOCADO SMASH**

2 ripe avocados

sea salt and freshly ground pepper

1 lime

1 lemon

1 orange

green salad, to serve

Preheat the oven to 375°F/180°C (convection 350°F/160°C). Get all your ingredients together.

Shred the spinach or greens and put into a large mixing bowl. Drain the beans and add to the bowl. Use a fork to mash the beans a little.

Cut the corn from the cob; when I do this I put it into a bowl and carefully cut the kernels off with a knife so they don't fly everywhere. Add the corn kernels to the beans and greens.

Finely chop the chile and cilantro—stalks and all—and add most of this to the bowl. Crack in the eggs. Season generously with salt and pepper.

Heat a dry frying pan and toast the cumin seeds for 30 seconds or so, then add these to the bowl too. Give it all a good mix.

Heat a little coconut oil in the pan over medium heat. Take heaped tablespoonfuls of the mixture and add them to the pan 3 or 4 at a time. You should get about 8 fritters. Fry for a couple of minutes, until golden brown on the bottom and set and golden around the edges, before flipping over.

Once the first batch are cooked, place them on a large baking sheet and pop them into the oven to keep warm while you cook the remaining fritters.

While the fritters are cooking, mash the avocados with a little salt and pepper. Use a knife to cut the peel from each of the citrus fruits. Cut each one into quarters, then cut out the pithy middle and coarsely chop the fruit, removing any big pieces of pith. Add to the avocado with the rest of the chile and cilantro and mix well.

Serve the fritters topped with the smashed avocado and some green salad.

# Butternut and sweet leek hash

This is my dream brunch. I can't get enough of it. So much so that I make it for lunch and dinner as well. Most Sunday nights when I was growing up, dinner would be Dad's fry-up—not the bacon-and-egg kind, but all our Sunday veggies crisped up to within an inch of its life—that amazing golden stuff that happens on the bottom of a pan.

It is a pan full of good things: burnished squash, sweet caramelized leeks, golden potatoes, and perfect sunshine eggs, topped off with a neat little herb-and-leek dressing that takes this hash to the next level. Though my dad would probably still have a spoonful of Branston pickle on the side.

This all happens in half an hour in the pan. It's also a great way to use up leftover cooked root vegetables, which would make it even quicker. If you are vegan, skip the cheese and eggs and use 3½ ounces/100 g of soaked cashews blended with ⅓ cup/100 ml of cold water in place of the yogurt. I make this for my family a lot, and it's really good this way too.

SERVES 2, OR 4 WITH EGGS

2 leeks

1 tablespoon coconut or olive oil

14 ounces/400 g new potatoes

½ medium butternut squash

a few fresh chives

a few sprigs of parsley

4 tablespoons crème fraîche or yogurt

½ lemon

sea salt and freshly ground pepper

a crumble of Lancashire or cheddar cheese (optional)

4 free-range or organic eggs (optional)

Fill and boil a kettle of water and get your ingredients together. Put a large nonstick pan over medium heat.

Wash the leeks, then finely slice them and add them to the pan with a little of the coconut oil. Stir every couple of minutes.

While the leeks are cooking, cut the potatoes into ½-inch/1-cm pieces and put them into a large saucepan. Pour over boiling water from the kettle and bring to a boil, then turn down the heat and simmer for 5 minutes.

Seed the squash and cut into pieces about the same size as the potatoes. Once the potatoes have had 5 minutes, add the squash to the pan of boiling

CONTINUED

water for a final 3 minutes of cooking. Once the potatoes and squash have had their time and have softened a little, drain them and leave in the colander to steam-dry a little.

Spoon 3 tablespoons of the leeks into a deep bowl. Turn the heat up under the leek pan, add a little more oil if necessary, then add the potatoes and squash and fry, turning every couple of minutes, but not too often—you want to allow each side enough time to build up a bit of a golden crust.

While potatoes and squash cook, chop the herbs and add them to the reserved 3 tablespoons of leeks. Add the crème fraîche or yogurt, the juice of half a lemon, and some salt and pepper, and blend well, using a handheld blender.

Keep turning the hash in the pan until it's all nicely golden. Now there are a couple of ways you can take it. Keep it like this—it's delicious as it is. Or crumble a little cheese over and allow it to melt in. Then crack the eggs into the pan, pop a lid on top, and allow to cook for 3 to 5 minutes, until the whites are set but the yolks are still runny.

Serve the hash with the leek-and-herb dressing scattered over. Stir it through before you eat.

# 30-minute sweet potato chili

Usually the joy of a pot of chili is that it builds up flavor for hours, but this one is different. It's a bit fresher and brighter, but it's still packed with flavor from the chipotle and spices and its chile-and-herb drizzle. Passata is puréed raw tomatoes, with seeds and skins strained out. If you can't find it, pass good canned tomatoes through a food mill or sieve.

SERVES 6

3 cups/750 ml passata

1 (14-ounce/400-g) can of Puy lentils

1 (14-ounce/400-g) can of adzuki beans

⅓ cup/50 g quinoa

1 to 2 tablespoons chipotle paste (depending on how hot you like things)

1 large sweet potato

a bunch of green onions (about 4 ounces/125 g)

2 cloves garlic

coconut or olive oil

1 tablespoon smoked paprika

1 tablespoon ground cumin

1 tablespoon ground coriander

1 (8-ounce/220-g) jar of roasted red peppers

TO SERVE

1 or 2 green chiles, seeded

a bunch of fresh cilantro

leaves from a few sprigs of oregano or thyme

1 lime

extra-virgin olive oil

sea salt

coconut yogurt or Greek yogurt

Get all your ingredients together and put both a large saucepan and a frying pan over medium heat.

Empty the passata, lentils, beans, and quinoa into the saucepan and add 1⅔ cups/400 ml of cold water. Add the chipotle paste and cook on the highest heat for 10 to 15 minutes.

Peel, quarter, and finely slice the sweet potato, coarsely slice the green onions, and peel the garlic. Put the green onions and sweet potato into the frying pan with a little coconut or olive oil and fry for 5 minutes. Add the smoked paprika and fry for a further 3 minutes.

Using a fine grater, grate the garlic cloves into the tomato-quinoa mixture. Stir in the cumin and coriander.

Take a ladleful of chili out of the saucepan and add it to the sweet potatoes in the frying pan. Stir it all around to get the goodness from the bottom of the pan, then pour it carefully into the chili pan. Simmer together for another 10 minutes with the lid on. Drain the red peppers, coarsely slice them, and add them to the chili pan.

While the chili is cooking, put the green chile and cilantro into a blender with the oregano or thyme, the juice of the lime, and 2 tablespoons of olive oil. Add 4 tablespoons of water and a pinch of salt and blend until smooth.

Serve the chili in deep bowls, topped with yogurt and the chile drizzle.

# Persian pea and herb bakes with beet labneh

I love the Persian way of eating: the spices, the sharing, and the sense of family. One of my best friends, Mersedeh, is from a family of incredible Persian cooks and I remember eating these little bakes, *kookoo shabzi*—a generously herbed kind of Persian frittata—at their family parties. I get my fix of these now at a great Persian stall on Broadway Market in Hackney, where *kookoos* are made in dainty little portions.

These are my version. I expect they veer a long way from the original (especially with the addition of peas), but they are my homage to Persian food and family in all its colorful, highly flavored glory. I've been told the key to a good *kookoo shabzi* is to use an equal amount of each herb so the flavors are balanced, and to gently cook the herbs first to release all their water. I serve them with a beet *labneh* (salted yogurt) and some salad greens and flatbreads.

I have purposely planned this recipe so that you have a few of these little *kookoos* left over, as I want you to try how great they are thrown into a wrap with some pickles and a drizzle of tahini for lunch the next day.

....................................................................................................................

Preheat the oven to 425°F/220°C (convection 400°F/200°C). Fill and boil a kettle of water and get all your ingredients and equipment together. Put a nonstick frying pan on the heat. You'll also need a nonstick 12-cup muffin pan.

Once the kettle has boiled, soak the saffron in a little boiling water (about 2 tablespoons/25 ml). Put the peas into a heatproof bowl and cover with more boiling water.

Finely chop the green onions, then finely chop all the herbs to a more or less even size. Heat a little oil in the hot frying pan and add the onions, all but a little pinch of the herbs, and all the ground coriander. Stir for 1 to 2 minutes, until softened and wilted.

## SERVES 4

### FOR THE BAKES
a good pinch of saffron strands
14 ounces/400 g frozen peas
4 green onions
a bunch of mint
a bunch of dill
a bunch of chives
a bunch of parsley
a little olive oil
1 heaping teaspoon ground coriander
6 free-range or organic eggs
1 green chile
sea salt and freshly ground pepper

### FOR THE BEET LABNEH
2 small cooked beets
½ cup/125ml Greek yogurt
sea salt
1 tablespoon tahini
1 unwaxed lemon
a small handful of chopped walnuts

### TO SERVE
warm flatbreads
salad greens

Whisk the eggs in a large mixing cup or bowl, then add the saffron liquid, drained peas, and the wilted herbs and green onions. Chop the chile finely and add that too; season with sea salt and pepper. Mix well.

Drizzle a tiny bit of oil into each cup of a 12-cup muffin pan and jiggle it around a bit to coat the sides. Pop the muffin pan into the oven for 30 seconds to warm up the oil. Then take the pan out of the oven and pour the batter into the cups to come two-thirds of the way up each. Place in the hot oven for 10 to 12 minutes, until cooked through and slightly golden.

While the bakes are cooking, grate the beets into a bowl. Add the yogurt, a really good pinch of salt, the tahini, and the zest and juice of the lemon. Mix well, then scatter the walnuts and the remaining herbs on top.

Serve two bakes each, with warm flatbreads, salad greens, and generous spoonfuls of the beet labneh.

# Squash, roasted tomato, and popped black bean salad

This salad is all about texture; not that it doesn't taste fantastic, but texture is one of the things I think we often forget about when we are putting a meal together. Here, it's crisp roast squash slices, soft roast tomatoes, and popped black beans, which add an amazingly crunchy, almost popcorn-like element.

Preheat the oven to 475°F/240°C (convection 450°F/220°C) and get all your ingredients together.

Halve and seed your squash and cut it into ½-inch/1-cm slices. Place them on a baking sheet and drizzle with a little oil, then sprinkle with salt, pepper, and the ground cardamom seeds. Place in the hot oven for 25 minutes, until blistered and golden, turning halfway through cooking.

Halve the cherry tomatoes and put them on another sheet. Grate over the peeled ginger and season with salt and pepper. Drizzle over a little oil and put into the oven with the squash; your tomatoes will take about 20 minutes.

Meanwhile, drain the black beans well and dry them on paper towels. Heat a large pan over medium heat, and once it's nice and hot, add the beans and dry-fry, turning from time to time, until they pop and turn crisp.

When the time is nearly up for your squash, take it out of the oven, scatter the coconut over the top, and put back into the oven for a couple of minutes to toast.

Mix the yogurt with the lime zest and juice and the ground cardamom seeds. Season with a little salt and pepper and mix well.

Take everything out of the oven and scatter over a big platter. Top with a drizzle of the cardamom yogurt and a little more lime if it's needed.

SERVES 4

1 butternut or other similar squash
olive or coconut oil
sea salt and freshly ground pepper
seeds from 1 cardamom pod, ground
10½ ounces/300 g cherry tomatoes
a thumb-size piece of ginger
1 (14-ounce/400-g) can of black beans
1¾ ounces/50 g flaked coconut

TO SERVE
⅓ cup/100 ml Greek or coconut yogurt
zest and juice of 1 unwaxed lime
seeds from 1 cardamom pod, ground
sea salt and freshly ground pepper

# 10 favorite suppers
# from 10 favorite vegetables

## BEETS

*Beet and kale sauté; serves 2*

Coarsely slice 4 cooked beets and sauté in olive oil for 10 minutes, until crisp • Add 2 handfuls of kale and wilt • Top with crumbled walnuts and, if you like, some goat cheese.

## BROCCOLINI

*Broccolini fry; serves 2*

Fry 2 large handfuls of broccolini in a little oil with some chile and soy sauce • Toss with the segments and a little juice from 2 oranges (blood oranges are my favorite) • Serve on top of steamed rice or noodles.

## POTATOES

*Potato cakes; serves 2*

Scrub and grate 8 ounces/250 g of potatoes and squeeze out the moisture • Add dill, 2 eggs, and a scattering of crumbly cheese, such as Lancashire • Form into little cakes and fry, in a little olive oil, for 4 minutes on each side • Serve with salad and lemon yogurt.

## GREENS

*Greens pasta; serves 2*

Shred a bunch of greens and sauté in olive oil with the zest of 1 lemon, 1 chopped red chile, and 1 clove of garlic • When greens have wilted, stir in 5 ounces/150 g of cooked pasta • Finish with (vegetarian) Parmesan or pecorino.

## CARROTS

*Quick soup; serves 2*

Finely chop 4 carrots and sauté with 1 red onion until soft • Add a can of chopped tomatoes, squeeze in the juice of 1 orange, and put in the orange halves • Simmer until the carrots are tender, remove the orange halves, then purée.

## ZUCCHINI

Zucchini and chickpea stew; serves 2

Finely slice a red onion and sauté in a little olive oil • Add 2 zucchini, sliced into discs the thickness of a nickel • Add a handful of halved red cherry tomatoes and cook for 10 minutes • Add a 14-ounce/400-g can of chickpeas, drained • Warm through and serve with bread.

## PEPPERS

Spicy roasted red peppers with eggs; serves 2

Take a jar of roasted red peppers and sauté them in olive oil with 1 chopped chile, 2 chopped tomatoes, and a pinch of cumin seeds • Once all is soft, break in 2 eggs and bake at 350°F/180°C (convection 325°F/160°C) for 12 minutes • Top with chopped parsley.

## CORN

Fresh corn fritters; serves 2

Cut kernels from 2 ears of corn • Mix with 1 egg, sea salt, black pepper, and 1 tablespoon of spelt flour • Add chopped red chile (optional) • Drop heaped tablespoons into a hot frying pan and fry for 2 minutes each side • Top with tomato chutney, salad leaves, and even some slices of halloumi.

## PEAS

Quick pea toasts; serves 2

Shell 2 pounds/1 kg of fresh peas or use 1 pound/500 g of frozen peas • Pour over boiling water and drain; purée with the juice of ½ a lemon and olive oil • Pile onto toast • Top with goat cheese or feta, or ribboned zucchini.

## SUGAR SNAP PEAS

Green lemon sauté; serves 2

Sauté 2 handfuls of sugar snap peas in olive oil with 2 big handfuls of broccoli florets and spinach, ½ clove garlic, and the zest and juice of 1 lemon • Serve with brown rice.

# Pan-roasted lime, feta, and chile greens burrito

This is a dream of a burrito. It's one of those glorious things that manages to balance hearty with fresh, spicy with sharp, smoky with sweet.

I don't like rice in my burrito—to me it's a filler. I'd rather pack it full of flash-fried greens with chile, avocado, and smoky lime-spiked beans, but if you are particularly hungry, then a scattering of cooked brown rice or quinoa would work here.

Get all your ingredients together. You will need two frying pans, one large and one medium.

Slice the garlic and chile and put them into a medium frying pan with a little coconut oil. Cook until starting to brown, then add the smoked paprika, the borlotti beans with their liquid, and the juice of one lime, and let it burble away for 10 minutes to heat through.

Coarsely chop the cherry tomatoes and mix them with the juice of half a lime and the chopped cilantro. Peel and pit the avocados and mash with the juice of the other half lime. Stem and shred the kale. Take the oregano leaves off their stems.

Grate the zest of a lime over the feta and scatter over a couple of large pinches of chile flakes. Put 1 teaspoon of coconut oil into a large frying pan and fry the feta over medium heat for 3 minutes each side, until just brown, being careful not to move it too much; otherwise it will break up.

Once the feta is browned on both sides, take it out of the pan and cover to keep warm. Cut into slices. Add the shredded kale and oregano to the

CONTINUED

## MAKES 4 BURRITOS

2 cloves garlic

1 red chile

coconut oil

½ teaspoon smoked paprika

1 (14-ounce/400-g) can
of borlotti beans

4 unwaxed limes

2 handfuls of cherry tomatoes

a small bunch of cilantro, chopped

2 ripe avocados

7 ounces/200 g baby kale
or spinach

leaves from a few sprigs of oregano

7 ounces/200 g feta cheese
or firm tofu

red chile flakes

4 large whole wheat or
seeded tortillas

same pan, with a little oil if needed, and add the zest of a lime, a good pinch of chile flakes, and 2 tablespoons of water. Cook away the water and sauté until starting to crisp.

Scoop the beans out of their pan into a serving bowl. When the greens are done, put them into another serving bowl and rinse out and dry the pan. Put it back over high heat and toast the tortillas in the dry pan. If you have a gas stove, you can also do this by holding each tortilla with tongs for a few seconds over the open flame.

Make your own burritos at the table. Lay each tortilla on a plate, leaving a bit of space at the top and bottom. Add the warm beans and top with the greens, a few slices of feta, a spoonful of the tomato salsa, and some mashed avocado. Fold the bottom and top of each tortilla over, then bring the sides in and roll the burrito up. Serve with any extra salsa and avocado.

# Grilled avocado barley bowl

This bowl sits at the crossroads of fresh and hearty. It's the kind of food I remember eating when I was growing up in San Francisco: light, bright, and goodness-packed. This dish is a teaming-up of all the things that remind me of California: unusual grains, bright citrus, avocado, nuts and seeds, and sprouted seeds and beans.

You can use any grain here—I like pearled barley for its chewy, pillowy heartiness, but quinoa, millet, or even brown rice would work great. If you are vegan, leave out the feta and use coconut yogurt. I have used basil, as I usually have a basil plant sitting on the windowsill, but any soft herb would be good.

This barley salad bowl is just as good the next day, and travels particularly well, so I often make it for plane journeys, or make extra for lunch the next day.

.......................................................................................................................

**SERVES 4**

1 cup/200 g red pearl barley

sea salt

zest and juice of
1½ unwaxed lemons

1¾ ounces/50 g almonds

1¾ ounces/50 g sunflower or pumpkin seeds

2 ripe avocados

leaves from a large bunch of basil

¾ cup/200 ml plain yogurt or coconut yogurt

freshly ground pepper

3½ ounces/100 g feta cheese

7 ounces/200 g spinach or other tender greens

Fill and boil a kettle of water and get all your ingredients together. Heat a grill pan over high heat.

First, get the pearled barley cooking. Rinse it well under cold water, then put it into a pan with twice the amount of water and a good pinch of salt. Squeeze in the juice of half a lemon, then put the squeezed lemon half into the pan. Cook for about 25 minutes.

Heat a frying pan over medium heat. Coarsely chop the almonds and toast them in the pan with the seeds until just turning golden brown.

Cut the avocados in half, discard the pits, then put them cut-side down on the grill pan and cook until they have nice griddle marks.

CONTINUED

Make a quick yogurt sauce: shred the basil leaves and mix with the yogurt, the zest and juice of the remaining lemon, and a good pinch each of salt and pepper in a small bowl.

Once the barley is cooked, drain any remaining water, then tumble it into a large dish, crumble over the feta cheese, and sprinkle with the toasted almonds and seeds. Shred the spinach, add to the dish, and mix well. Season with salt and pepper, remembering that the feta is quite salty.

Serve the barley topped with half a warm avocado ready to spoon out of its peel, big helpings of yogurt sauce, and more basil, if needed.

# Sweet roasted zucchini with crispy chickpeas

This is a very quick and insanely good version of a ratatouille, which was a classic in my house growing up. I use the broiler instead of the oven to cook the zucchini quickly and to impart maximum smoky-sweet flavor.

I eat this on its own with salad and some quinoa or bread, but if you want to make it a hearty meal, you could add some grilled halloumi or baked ricotta (see page 90). Leftovers are amazing in sandwiches or an omelet.

Preheat your broiler to high and get all your ingredients and equipment together. For this recipe, it really speeds things up to have a food processor with a grating attachment. If not, a box grater will do.

Grate the zucchini then scatter evenly on a rimmed baking sheet, season with salt and pepper, drizzle with a little oil, and place under the broiler to cook and char for about 20 minutes, turning every couple of minutes.

Meanwhile, put a frying pan over medium heat. Thinly slice the red onion and add it to the pan with a splash of olive oil and the thyme leaves. Cook for 5 minutes, until soft and sweet.

Finely chop the red peppers and tomatoes and finely slice the garlic. Once the onions are browned, add them to the pan of zucchini with the peppers, tomatoes, and garlic and continue to cook and brown, turning every 5 minutes, for a further 10 to 15 minutes.

Put the frying pan back over high heat and add a little more olive oil. Add the chickpeas, a good pinch of salt and pepper, and the zest of the lemon, and cook until the chickpeas are crisped around the edges. This will take about 10 minutes, and you'll need to keep tossing the chickpeas in the pan.

Once the zucchini mixture is softened and sweet and charred in places, scatter the chickpeas over it. Serve with some lemon-dressed greens.

SERVES 4

4 medium zucchini
sea salt and freshly ground pepper
olive oil
1 red onion
leaves from ½ bunch of thyme
1 (8-ounce/230-g) jar of roasted red peppers
1¼ pounds/550 g cherry tomatoes
2 cloves garlic
1 (14-ounce/400-g) can of chickpeas, or 1½ cups/250 g home-cooked chickpeas (see pages 241–245)
1 unwaxed lemon

TO SERVE
lemon-dressed greens

# 10 simple baked potatoes

**SWEET POTATO**

Wash and dry 2 sweet potatoes, each weighing 8 to 10 ounces/ 250 to 300 g, and prick them with a fork. Roast them at 425°F/220°C (convection 400°F/200°C) for 30 to 45 minutes, until soft throughout. **FOR 2 POTATOES:**

**1**

**PURÉE** 2 tomatoes, 1 chile, a bunch of cilantro. **HEAT** black beans, 1 clove garlic, chile, pinch of cinnamon. **TOP WITH** beans, chile sauce, mashed avocado.

**2**

**SAUTÉ** a couple of handfuls of spinach. **CHOP** sun-dried tomatoes. **SLICE** avocado. **TOP WITH** hummus, spinach, tomatoes, avocado, lemon juice.

**3**

**WARM** 1 can of lima beans, pinch of smoked paprika, leaves from a few sprigs of thyme, lemon zest. **CHOP** parsley. **TOP WITH** warm beans, chopped parsley, grating of Manchego.

**4**

**PAN-FRY** 1 can of drained chickpeas in a little oil, with a teaspoon of cumin, until crisp. **ADD** chopped roasted peppers, cherry tomatoes, parsley, basil, lemon zest. **PILE** onto potatoes and crumble feta over the top.

**5**

**HALVE** potatoes and scoop out flesh. **MIX WITH** a handful of grated cheddar, sautéed leeks, chopped chives, shredded greens. **PILE** back into skins. **TOP WITH** more cheese. **GRILL** until melted (4 to 5 minutes). **SERVE** with yogurt, mixed with lemon juice and chives.

## REGULAR POTATO

Wash and dry 2 floury potatoes (russets), each weighing about 10 to 14 ounces/300 to 400 g, then prick, rub with oil and salt, and bake at 425°F/220°C (convection 400°F/200°C) for 1 hour. **FOR 2 POTATOES:**

**6**

CHOP 6 cornichons, ½ a bunch of parsley, 2 tablespoons capers, zest of 1 lemon. **MIX WITH** 1 tablespoon crème fraîche or Greek yogurt, salt, pepper. **MASH** into potatoes. **TOP WITH** arugula.

**7**

COOK 1 can of white beans. **ADD** leaves from a sprig of thyme, pinch of dried chile, salt. **TOP WITH** beans, grated cheddar, chile sauce.

**8**

CHOP FINELY ½ a cabbage, ½ a bunch of parsley, 1 apple. **GRATE** 1 carrot. **CHOP** 1 red onion, scrunch with juice of ½ lemon and salt. **MIX** 1 tablespoon yogurt, juice of ½ lemon. **PILE** onto potatoes.

**9**

COOK 1 sliced leek until soft, add greens and wilt, add leaves from 2 sprigs of thyme. **STIR IN** 1 tablespoon whole-grain mustard, 2 tablespoons grated cheddar. **TOP WITH** leeks and cheese.

**10**

COOK 1 tablespoon mustard seeds with a handful of curry leaves until they pop. **ADD** a handful of spinach and chopped green onions. **COOK** for 5 minutes. **ADD** zest of a lemon.

# Charred mushroom and cashew pizza

**MAKES 2 LARGE PIZZAS**

**FOR THE MUSHROOMS**
1 red onion
olive oil
9 ounces/250 g mushrooms
1 clove garlic
leaves from a few sprigs of thyme

**FOR THE CASHEW RICOTTA**
7 ounces/200 g cashews
juice of ½ unwaxed lemon
1 clove garlic
a pinch of fennel seeds
1 tablespoon olive oil
1 tablespoon nutritional yeast
(optional)

**FOR THE PIZZA**
2½ cups/300 g light spelt flour
⅔ cup/150 ml tepid water
sea salt
1 tablespoon olive oil, plus
more for cooking
½ cup tomato passata
(see page 117)
a handful of small black olives,
pitted
a small handful of arugula

My vegan brother, Owen, regularly puts in requests for things he misses from the old days. Most frequently he asks for banoffee pie or a really good pizza, and this is what I make him. I love cooking and eating vegan food—it leaves me feeling light and bright, and I relish how it makes me rethink my cooking because it takes a little more attention.

If vegan cooking can sometimes be considered time-consuming and complicated, or worthy and uninteresting, pizza proves that's not the case. This pizza topping also works amazingly on my cauliflower pizza base from *A Modern Way to Eat*, which is a good gluten-free alternative. I use a little nutritional yeast here with the cashews, as it adds depth and is packed with nutrients, but if you can't find it, don't worry, you can just leave it out.

Nutritional yeast is a deactivated yeast. As its rather matter-of-fact name suggests, it is jam-packed with vitamins, particularly B vitamins such as B12, which can be hard to come by in a vegan diet. It's also packed with folic acid, selenium, zinc, and protein. But more than anything I like it for its flavor: deeply savory and umami.

Get all your ingredients together and find yourself a large, heavy-bottomed frying pan—you'll need it to be around 10 inches/26 cm. Preheat your broiler to maximum.

To make the mushrooms, slice the red onion and put it into the frying pan with a little oil. Tear the mushrooms into pieces and coarsely chop the garlic, then add to the pan with the thyme leaves and cook for 4 to 5 minutes, turning every so often, until the mushrooms are charred and crispy and cooked through. Remove and put aside for later.

CONTINUED

Next, make the cashew ricotta: put all the ingredients into the bowl of a food processor with 3 tablespoons of cold water and blend until completely smooth—this should take 2 to 5 minutes, depending on how powerful your machine is. It should be the consistency of regular ricotta. Scoop out into a bowl and wash the processor bowl.

Now make the dough. Put the flour and water into the food processor with a good pinch of salt and a tablespoon of olive oil and pulse until the dough comes together in a ball. Tip it out and bring it together in your hands.

Put your frying pan over medium-to-high heat. If you have two pans about the right size, you can do both the pizzas at once; otherwise you can do one after the other, as they cook quickly. Cut the dough into two equal halves and cover one half for later. Put the other half onto a floured work surface and use a rolling pin to roll it out into a ½-inch/1-cm-thick circle about the size of your frying pan.

Drizzle a little oil into the hot pan, then carefully lift in the dough. Leave it on the heat for about 3 minutes, so that the bottom is starting to cook, while you quickly top the pizza.

Spoon half the tomato passata over, then the mushrooms. Dot with the cashew cheese and the olives.

Pop the pizza under the broiler for 4 to 5 minutes, until it is cooked through and the cashew cheese is browned. Repeat with the second pizza.

To finish, strew with some arugula leaves and cut into generous slices. Homemade bliss.

# Smoky corn chowder with maple-toasted coconut

I spent my very first few years living just outside San Francisco. I remember glee-filled trips to the city over the big red bridge—it seemed like a wonderland. These trips were always fueled, at my request, by Shirley Temples (lemonade and grenadine—a lurid pink glass full of dreams) and deep bowls of chowder, sometimes in hollowed-out sourdough *boules*, which, as a little girl, I thought were amazing and very posh.

I still think a good chowder takes a lot of beating for something comforting and nourishing. This is my new version, a warming blanket of a soup topped with smoky spice and some maple-toasted coconut.

I use some smoked salt here to amp up the smoky flavor. The best stuff, Halen Môn, is made and smoked on Anglesey, where I spend a lot of time and where my partner, John, is from. If you don't have smoked salt, don't worry; your usual sea salt will do just fine.

......................................................................................................................

Preheat the oven to 400°F/200°C (convection 375°F/180°C). Fill and boil a kettle of water and get all your ingredients together. Put a griddle pan over high heat.

Peel and chop the onion and celery finely and put them into a large saucepan with a tablespoon of oil. Cook for 5 minutes, until soft and sweet.

While this is happening, put the corn on the hot griddle and char on all sides, turning every minute or so.

Keeping an eye on the corn, peel the sweet potato and chop it into ½-inch/ 1-cm chunks. Add these to the onion and celery with a good pinch of smoked salt. Pour in 5 cups/1.25 liters of hot water from the kettle, add the stock

⠿ CONTINUED

## SERVES 4 TO 6

1 onion

1 celery stalk

coconut or olive oil

2 ears corn

1 medium sweet potato

smoked salt or sea salt

1 tablespoon vegetable stock powder or ½ stock cube

½ large cauliflower

2 limes

### FOR THE COCONUT TOPPING

a handful of coconut flakes

1 tablespoon maple syrup

1 teaspoon smoked paprika

### TO SERVE

good olive oil

sea salt and freshly ground pepper

some chopped herbs—parsley, cilantro, or cress

powder, and bring to a simmer. Coarsely chop the cauliflower, add to the soup, and simmer until the sweet potato is almost cooked.

Meanwhile, check your corn and keep turning until it is all charred.

Cover a baking sheet with parchment paper and scatter the coconut flakes on the baking sheet with the maple syrup and smoked paprika and toast in the oven until golden; this will take 4 to 5 minutes.

Once the corn is charred on all sides, take it off the heat and allow it to cool before cutting the kernels from the cob—when I do this, I rest the corn in a bowl so the kernels don't go everywhere.

Add half the corn to the soup and purée with a handheld blender until really creamy and smooth. Squeeze in the juice of the limes, season well, and serve topped with the remaining charred corn, the toasted coconut, some olive oil, and herbs or cress.

# Green bean and chile paneer

This is a super-quick but supremely flavorful curry that fills my house with incredible smells. It's spicy, sticky, and sweet and, for me, that's the best way to eat paneer. Its roots lie in Kashmir, a place I have never been to but somewhere my parents visited when they were young. They often tell me of its beauty, and I imagine it while scooping up this flavor-packed, cloudlike paneer.

I show you how to make your own paneer on page 248. It's really simple, and it is a great vegetarian staple that can be used in most of the dishes where you would use tofu. If you use store-bought (which I often do), it's best to soak it in a little water for 5 minutes first—this will help it become more cloudlike and it will soak up the flavors better. Kashmiri chile is available in Indian shops and good spice shops.

Vegans can make this with firm tofu and it is just as amazing. Serve with warm chapatis or flatbreads for scooping, mango chutney, and some rice if you are really hungry (the cauliflower rice on page 88 works well).

.......................................................................................................

Get all your ingredients together. If you're using store-bought paneer, put the paneer in a bowl of water and leave to soak.

Finely chop the onion and garlic. Put the coconut oil into a heavy-bottomed pan and place over medium heat, then add the onion and garlic and cook for about 5 minutes, until soft and sweet and beginning to brown.

Trim the tops from your green beans.

Add all the dry spices to the pan, then turn the heat to low, and stir for a little while to toast the spices and release their flavors.

CONTINUED

## SERVES 4

1 medium onion

3 cloves garlic

2 tablespoons coconut oil

17 ounces/500 g green beans

1 tablespoon cumin seeds

1 teaspoon ground turmeric

1 teaspoon Kashmiri chile
or mild chile powder

1 heaping teaspoon ground
coriander

4 vine-ripe tomatoes, or 7 ounces/
200 g cherry tomatoes

a thumb-size piece fresh ginger

1 lemon

1 tablespoon runny honey

1 red chile

7 ounces/200 g paneer

## TO SERVE

sea salt

1 lemon

a small bunch of cilantro

Coarsely chop the tomatoes and peel and coarsely chop the ginger. Add them to the pan and cook for another 2 to 3 minutes over high heat.

Add the green beans to the pan along with the juice of the lemon and the honey, and stir to coat them with the spices. Add a scant cup/100 ml of water and cook until the beans have lost their rawness, all the water has evaporated, and everything is well coated. This will take about 4 minutes.

Finely chop the red chile. Drain the paneer and coarsely cut into ¾-inch/ 2-cm slices. Add them to the pan and stir to coat with all the tomatoes and spices.

Season well with sea salt. Squeeze over the juice of the lemon, then chop the cilantro and scatter it over.

# Rye pancakes with crispy sunchokes

These are deliciously savory rye pancakes that I top with some flash-fried sunhokes, but outside of their short season some new potatoes will do just as well. I often make a double batch and store them in the fridge to use throughout the week for quesadillas and burritos.

If you don't buy rye flour often, do think about trying it here. It makes a rich, filling, and super-satisfying bread (see page 254), and it's great in brownies and any other chocolate baking.

........................................................................................................................

Get all your ingredients and equipment together. You'll need a large nonstick frying pan.

To make the batter, combine the flours and salt in a bowl. Use a fork to stir in the eggs until the batter is raggedy, then gradually whisk in the water. The batter may seem a bit thin, but it will thicken as it rests for 5 minutes while you get on with the toppings.

Use a mandoline or your excellent knife skills to very finely slice the sunchokes or potatoes (there is no need to peel). Finely chop the green onions.

Heat a tablespoon of olive oil in a large frying pan over high heat and add the drained capers. Leave to cook for 4 minutes, until crispy, then scoop out with a slotted spoon and leave to one side.

Leave the pan on the heat and add the sunchoke slices. Fry them over high heat, turning every so often, for about 10 minutes, or until they are starting to crisp and becoming golden. Add the green onions and fry for a further 3 minutes, then grate over the zest of the lemon and add the juice of half the lemon. Place over low heat while you make the pancakes.

CONTINUED

**SERVES 4**
**(MAKES 8 TO 10 PANCAKES)**

**FOR THE PANCAKES**
¾ cup/110 g rye flour
½ cup/100 g spelt flour
a good pinch of sea salt
3 free-range or organic eggs
2 cups/500 ml water,
plus more if needed
olive oil

**FOR THE TOPPING**
14 ounces/400 g sunchokes
or new potatoes
4 green onions
olive oil
2 tablespoons capers, drained
1 unwaxed lemon
7 ounces/200 g ricotta cheese
2 ounces/60 g arugula
1 red chile, chopped (optional)

Turn your oven to low. Heat a medium frying pan over medium heat. Rub the pan with a touch of oil, then pour in just enough batter to thinly coat the bottom. As you pour, rotate the pan so the batter runs to cover the entire bottom of the pan. Cook for a couple of minutes, until the pancake is browned, then flip with a spatula to brown the second side. Stack the pancakes on a plate as you make them and keep them warm in the oven.

Serve topped with the sunchokes and crispy capers, and crumble over the ricotta. Scatter over the arugula and finish with a final squeeze of lemon juice and, if you like, some chopped red chile.

# Winter chopped salad with candied seeds

Two things seem to happen around the same day in late summer: I start wearing socks and I stop eating salads. When I say I stop, I mean I stop being able to find them a satisfying meal, not that I don't let a single piece of arugula pass my lips until the sun comes out again. This salad is the exception. It's pretty much all raw and flavor-packed, but it comes with such a feeling of autumn that I relish it even when the woolly hats come out. I use a variety of different-colored carrots and beets to keep things interesting. Search them out if you can—they make this salad incredibly beautiful. Serve with flatbreads and a crumbling of feta or some torn mozzarella for a main meal.

SERVES 4 AS A MAIN DISH OR 6 AS PART OF A MEAL

FOR THE SALAD

3 carrots

3 beets

1 romaine lettuce or a head of winter greens

1 pear

a handful of pecans

a handful of pumpkin seeds

a splash of maple syrup

sea salt and freshly ground pepper

1¾ ounces/50 g pecorino cheese (optional)

FOR THE DRESSING

3 tablespoons olive oil

zest and juice of 1 unwaxed lemon

1 tablespoon tahini

1 tablespoon red wine vinegar

Get all your ingredients together.

Peel, chop, and slice all the vegetables and the pear as thinly as you can, making sure to shred the greens or lettuce especially thinly; a mandoline may be useful here, but a sharp knife will do just as well.

Put a sheet of parchment paper on a small tray or a plate, then put the nuts into a frying pan. Toast briefly, then add the seeds and toast until the seeds smell toasted and are starting to brown. Add the maple syrup and a pinch of salt and stir, then take off the heat, tip onto the parchment and leave to cool.

Mix all the dressing ingredients in a little jar.

Put all the chopped veggies into a bowl, season with salt and pepper, pour in the dressing, and mix well. Shave the pecorino on top, if using, and scatter with the nuts and seeds.

forty-
minute
feasts

These feasts take a little longer, but as they come together in about forty minutes, they are easily achievable on a weekday. They have a few more ingredients than the quicker recipes, and the little bit of extra time often allows more depth and complexity of flavor to develop: lemon-scented *polpette*, a mushroom meze feast, slow-cooked tomato lentils, Buddha bowls of goodness, rainbow root vegetable tacos, deeply scented *pho*, homemade chickpea pasta, avocado and fries, sweet potato gnocchi pillows, frying pan pies, and throw-it-in-the-oven gratins.

# A grilled mushroom feast

This dish is one of the things I like to cook when people come for dinner. It's an unexpected riot of flavor and color, with lots of interesting, unique elements that sing when eaten together.

A long time ago, a brilliant Italian chef taught me to be brave with heat when it came to mushrooms: a hot pan, not overcrowded, with generous seasoning. And luckily, this way of cooking mushrooms is so well suited to speedy cooking. This is how I like mushrooms best: charred, dense, and smoky all at once. Marinating the mushrooms while the griddle heats up is a quick way to get some extra flavor into them. If you don't have a grill pan, you can use a large frying pan, or, even better, a barbecue grill.

Fill and boil a kettle of water and get all your ingredients together. Heat a grill pan.

Weigh out the rice in a mug or measuring cup, making a note of the level it comes up to, then rinse it in cold water and put it into the pan. Fill the mug to the same level with hot water from the kettle and add to the pan, then repeat so you have double the volume of water as rice. Put a lid on the pan and bring back to a boil, then turn down the heat and simmer for 30 to 35 minutes for black rice and about 20 for wild rice. Soak the currants in the white wine vinegar.

Break or chop any large mushrooms into thick slices, put them into a bowl, then add the paprika, maple syrup, lemon juice, sumac, and olive oil and mix well.

To make the tzatziki, grate the cucumber into a bowl. Toast the cumin and fennel seeds in a dry pan and add them to the cucumber, then stir in the yogurt, the lemon juice, and a good pinch each of salt and pepper and set aside.

⋯ CONTINUED

## SERVES 4

### FOR THE RICE
1¼ cups/200 g black or wild rice

3 tablespoons currants

2 tablespoons white wine vinegar

½ small bunch of dill and/or tarragon

### FOR THE MARINATED MUSHROOMS
1¾ pounds/800 g interesting mushrooms: king oyster, portobello, chestnut

2 teaspoons smoked paprika

2 tablespoons maple syrup or runny honey

juice of ½ lemon

2 tablespoons sumac

a good glug of olive oil

### FOR THE TZATZIKI
½ cucumber

½ teaspoon cumin seeds

½ teaspoon fennel seeds

⅔ cup/150 ml yogurt of your choice (I use coconut or Greek)

juice of ½ lemon

sea salt and freshly ground pepper

INGREDIENTS CONTINUED →

FOR THE HUMMUS
1 teaspoon coriander seeds
8 tablespoons homemade
or good store-bought hummus
sea salt and freshly ground pepper
seeds from ½ pomegranate

FOR THE OLIVE SALSA
a handful of black olives (I use Kalamata)
a small bunch of cilantro
sea salt and freshly ground pepper
olive oil

TO SERVE
flatbreads

Turn the oven on to low. Once the grill pan is smoking, add a layer of mushrooms and grill on all sides until charred, crispy, and cooked through. Work in batches rather than overcrowding the pan, as otherwise they won't cook properly. Keep one eye on the mushrooms, turning them as you need to, while you get on with another couple of jobs. Keep the first couple of batches warm in the low oven while you cook the rest.

Toast the coriander seeds in a dry pan and bash them with a mortar and pestle until you have a coarse powder, then add to the hummus with some more salt and freshly ground pepper if needed. Sprinkle with the pomegranate seeds.

Pit the olives and chop them and the cilantro together on a board until you have a coarse salsa. Scoop into a bowl, season with salt and pepper, then add a little drizzle of oil and put to one side.

Once the rice is cooked, drain any excess water, then mix in the currants and their soaking liquid along with a good pinch of salt and pepper. Chop the dill and tarragon and mix into the rice.

Once all the mushrooms are cooked, pile the rice onto plates, scatter the mushrooms on top, and serve with big spoonfuls of the olive salsa, hummus, and tzatziki. And, if you like, some flatbreads.

# Spinach and lemon polpette

These are lovely, light spinach and nutmeg *polpette* (meatballs) to serve with spaghetti and a quick tomato sauce. But if you want a lighter meal, they are just as good with some quinoa and a shock of green salad.

I use vegetarian-friendly Parmesan here, but if you can't get your hands on that, any vegetarian hard cheese will do the trick. For vegans, a spoonful of nutritional yeast will echo the flavor of the Parmesan, but you will need to add a few more bread crumbs or oats.

SERVES 4

FOR THE SPINACH POLPETTE
9 ounces/250 g spinach
½ cup/100 g cooked Puy lentils
1 free-range or organic egg
a good grating of nutmeg
1¾ ounces/50 g whole wheat bread crumbs or oats
1¾ ounces/50 g Parmesan cheese, (I use a vegetarian one) plus more to serve
zest of 1 unwaxed lemon
sea salt and freshly ground pepper
1 clove garlic

FOR THE SAUCE
a handful of almonds
2 cloves garlic
3 tablespoons olive oil
1 lemon
leaves from a small bunch of basil
12 ounces/350 g cherry tomatoes
sea salt and freshly ground pepper

10 ounces/300 g spaghetti of your choice (I use whole wheat)

Preheat the oven to 400°F/200°C (convection 375°F/180°C). Fill and boil a kettle of water and get all your ingredients together.

Wash the spinach and remove any tough stalks. Place a large frying pan over high heat and, when it's hot, add the spinach and dry fry until wilted and any water has evaporated.

Drain the lentils well if you are using canned, then put them into a blender and blend until they are mushy. Add the egg, nutmeg, bread crumbs, Parmesan, lemon zest, and some salt and pepper. Chop the garlic and add this too. Blend until combined, then remove from the blender and fold in the spinach.

Divide the mixture into four. From each quarter, make eight small balls. You should end up with 32 balls, each about 1 inch/2.5 cm. Place on a baking sheet and put into the oven for 15 to 20 minutes, until crisp and golden.

To make the sauce, put the almonds, garlic, and olive oil in a food processor. Pulse to a coarse texture then add the zest and juice of the lemon, the basil

CONTINUED

leaves, and the cherry tomatoes. Pulse again until you have a coarse pesto, then season well with salt and pepper.

When the polpette have had 10 minutes, fill a large pan with boiling water, add salt, and once it's at a rolling boil add the pasta and cook according to the package instructions (usually about 8 minutes).

Once the pasta is cooked, drain it, reserving some of the cooking liquid. Add the pesto and mix well, adding a little of the reserved pasta water to loosen if needed. Tangle the tomatoey pasta into bowls and top with the spinach polpette and a little more Parmesan, if you like.

# Silver Lake sweet potato bake

I wrote almost half this book at my sister's house in Silver Lake, Los Angeles. Smack bang in the middle of my stay was Thanksgiving, and the whole Jones clan were, by chance, together. It's not something we've ever celebrated, but in true Jones spirit we joined in, made a huge spread, and ate it with all our L.A. friends. We ate a mixture of recipes I'd been busy testing and tweaking and a few American classics we wanted an excuse to try out.

Ever since I was little I have been fascinated by the sweet potato casserole that graces the table at Thanksgiving, and how could you blame me? It's a sweet-toothed little girl's dream—whipped-up, sweetened mashed potato topped with burnished marshmallows, disguised as a savory dish, and legitimately eaten with your dinner. Weird and wonderful in equal measure.

This is my version, which is a long way from the original: way less sweet (no marshmallows), but with sweet potatoes, herbs, and a crunchy pecan topping. I now eat this regularly for my dinner, with a simple, super-lemony green salad to cut through the natural sweetness of the sweet potatoes.

SERVES 4

sea salt

4 medium sweet potatoes

2 leeks

olive oil or coconut oil

leaves from a few sprigs of sage

leaves from a few sprigs of thyme

2 large handfuls of spinach
(about 5 ounces/150 g)

freshly grated nutmeg

FOR THE TOPPING

2 slices of good bread or
2 handfuls of rolled oats

a handful of pecans
(about 1¾ ounces/50 g)

leaves from a few more sprigs
of thyme

2 tablespoons olive oil or coconut oil

1 tablespoon maple syrup

zest of 1 unwaxed lemon

sea salt and freshly ground pepper

FOR THE CASHEW CREAM

3½ ounces/100 g unsalted cashews

1¼ cups/300 ml unsweetened
almond milk

Preheat your oven to 425°F/220°C (convection 400°F/200°C). Fill and boil a kettle of water and get all your ingredients and equipment together. You will need a medium ovenproof baking dish, the kind you might use for a family lasagne.

Place a frying pan over high heat. Put a large saucepan on the heat and fill it with boiling water from the kettle. Add a pinch of salt.

Cut the sweet potatoes into ¼-inch/5-mm-thick slices (there is no need to peel). Halve, wash, and finely slice the leeks. Once the water is boiling, add the sweet potatoes, bring back to a boil, and cook for 10 minutes, until soft and cooked through but not falling apart.

Put the leeks into the frying pan with a little oil. Coarsely chop the sage leaves and add to the pan with the leaves from the thyme, then fry over medium heat for about 10 minutes, until soft and sweet.

Meanwhile, make the topping. Put the bread or oats into a food processor and pulse until you have crumbs, then add the pecans and thyme leaves and pulse again until the nuts are about the same size as the bread crumbs. Add the oil, maple syrup, and lemon zest, season well, and put to one side.

To make the cashew cream, blend the cashews until smooth and then add the almond milk and blend together until you have a really smooth cream.

Wash the spinach and remove any tough stalks. Once the leeks are soft and sweet, add the spinach and cook for a couple of minutes until it has wilted. Drain the sweet potatoes and tumble them into a baking dish, then spread the leeks and spinach on top. Grate in a little nutmeg, season well with salt and pepper, and evenly pour the cashew cream over it.

Scatter with the bread crumb topping and put into the oven to roast for 25 minutes, until golden brown.

# My favorite lentils with roasted tomatoes and horseradish

FOR THE LENTILS

1½ cups/300 g Puy lentils, washed

4 cloves garlic, unpeeled

1 small tomato

a few sprigs of thyme

2 bay leaves

1 tablespoon vegetable stock powder or ½ stock cube

a splash of red wine vinegar

FOR THE TOMATOES

14 ounces/400 g grape tomatoes or cherry tomatoes

sea salt and freshly ground pepper

zest of 1 unwaxed lemon

olive oil

a couple of handfuls of whole wheat bread crumbs

leaves from a small bunch of thyme

1 clove garlic, coarsely chopped

FOR THE HORSERADISH SAUCE

2 teaspoons jarred grated horseradish

½ cup/100 ml cottage cheese

Lentils pair so well with tomatoes, and the shock of fiery horseradish and the crisp savory crumb make this a firmly British dish. I like to serve this with some simple lemon-and-oil-dressed leaves.

Puy lentils lend themselves amazingly to quick cooking—they don't need soaking, they cook in 30 minutes, and they're hearty, delicious, and creamy. Adding a tomato and a few cloves of garlic to the pan as the lentils cook imparts great flavor. This way with lentils was taught to me by my old friend and longtime boss Jamie Oliver, but I'm pretty sure it's a classic Italian recipe. You will never want to eat lentils any other way.

If you do have time to soak the lentils overnight, it will make them easier to digest. I always try to remember, but if you've forgotten or don't have time it's not the end of the world. I use jarred grated horseradish here, not the creamed kind or the sauce, and the fresh stuff of course works well too. Make this vegan by using a vegan mayo or cream cheese instead of the cottage cheese.

Preheat the oven to 425°F/220°C (convection 400°F/200°C). Fill and boil a kettle of water and get all your ingredients together. You'll need a big pan for your lentils.

Put the lentils into the pan with the unpeeled garlic, whole tomato, thyme sprigs, bay leaves, and the stock powder. Cover with 1 quart/1 liter of boiling water, place over medium heat, bring to a simmer, then turn the heat down. Simmer for 25 to 30 minutes, until the lentils are soft and the water has evaporated. If they are looking too dry, top up with a little more boiling water from the kettle.

CONTINUED

Meanwhile, roast the tomatoes. Cut them in half and put them cut side up on a baking sheet with some salt and pepper and the zest of the lemon. Drizzle them with a little olive oil and put into the oven to roast for 15 minutes. On another baking sheet, mix the bread crumbs with the thyme leaves and coarsely chopped garlic and drizzle with oil. Season with a little salt and pepper and put to one side.

Mix the horseradish with the cottage cheese and set aside.

Once the tomatoes have had 15 minutes, put the sheet of bread crumbs into the oven and cook both for 5 minutes more.

By now the lentils should be cooked and all the water should have evaporated; scoop out the tomato and the garlic cloves and put them into a bowl. Once the garlic is cool enough to handle, pop the cloves out of their skins and use a fork to mash them to a paste with the tomato. Stir this paste back into the lentils. Taste, season with salt and pepper, then dress with a generous glug of olive oil and a splash of red wine vinegar.

Once the tomatoes are sticky and the bread crumbs are crisp, take everything out of the oven. Serve in deep bowls—a generous ladle of lentils topped with the tomatoes, horseradish sauce, and, finally, a scattering of bread crumbs.

# Curry leaf and smoky celery root pilaf

Kedgeree has long been our Christmas Day breakfast—the waft of spices and the cheery yellow of the eggs feel celebratory—but we eat it for dinner all year round.

Back in India, it was originally a vegetarian dish of lentils and rice; the smoked fish and eggs were only added to suit British tastes. I like the mix of smoke with the spice, so I roast celery root with smoked salt and stir it through; I use Anglesey's Halen Môn smoked salt, but if you can't find it, normal sea salt will do. I keep my eggs pretty runny, but if you like them firm, boil them for another minute or two.

To make this vegan, as I do for my brother and sister, leave out the eggs and use oil, not butter. If you can't find curry leaves, it will still be delicious without them.

**SERVES 6**

1 large celery root
coconut oil, butter, or ghee
smoked or regular sea salt
freshly ground pepper
2 onions
2 cloves garlic
2 green chiles
2 bay leaves
20 curry leaves (optional)
8 cardamom pods, bashed
3 teaspoons coriander seeds
3 teaspoons ground turmeric
2 cups/400 g basmati rice
6 free-range or organic eggs
8 tablespoons Greek yogurt
juice of 2 lemons
a bunch of parsley
a bunch of cilantro

Preheat the oven to 400°F/200°C (convection 375°F/180°C). Get all your ingredients and equipment together. Fill and boil a kettle of water.

Thickly peel the celery root, getting rid of any green bits, and cut it into ¾-inch/2-cm pieces. Put it on a baking sheet with a dollop of coconut oil or butter, a hefty pinch of smoked salt, and a good grind of pepper, and roast for 30 minutes, until tender.

Finely chop the onions and slice the garlic and chiles. Heat a good dollop of coconut oil, butter, or ghee in a large ovenproof pan with a lid. Add the onions, garlic, and bay and curry leaves, and cook over low heat for 10 minutes, until soft and sweet. Add the bashed cardamom pods and coriander seeds, the turmeric, chiles, and a couple of hearty pinches of

CONTINUED

smoked salt and stir for another 3 to 4 minutes over medium heat until the spices smell great. Take a tablespoonful of the onion mixture out of the pan and put aside for later.

Turn the heat up, add the rice and a little more oil if needed, and stir to coat with the oil and spices. Pour in 1 quart/1 liter of boiling water from the kettle—you want the water to come about ¾ inch/1 cm above the rice, so you may need a little more or a little less. Bring to a simmer. Put the lid on and put the whole thing into the oven for 20 to 25 minutes.

While the rice is cooking, boil the eggs. I boil my eggs in a pan of boiling water for 6 minutes for runny yolks, but cook a little longer if you like them firmer. Cool the eggs in cold water to stop the cooking, then peel and keep to one side.

Mix the yogurt with a squeeze of lemon, a pinch of smoked salt, and the spoonful of spices and onions you set aside earlier.

Once the celery root and rice have had their time, take them both out of the oven and stir the celery root into the fluffy rice along with the chopped herbs and the rest of the lemon juice. Cut the eggs in half and lay them on top, then pop the lid back on to keep everything warm. Serve in the middle of the table, with the yogurt for spooning over.

# Buddha bowls

This is a knockout, a Rocky Balboa of a dish: a heady, peanut-spiked curry topped with a bright carrot pickle, crispy kale, and a scattering of toasted seeds.

It is based on a brilliant, nourishing bowl I ate at a very gray Glastonbury Festival. Knee-deep in mud, wet through after hours of biblical rain, I was getting a bit grumpy with hunger and was in need of some proper nourishment. These Buddha bowls came to my rescue. This is the version I make at home, which I love. It will taste best when eaten in the rain, in a field, after walking in circles for at least an hour.

This all comes together in 45 minutes, but you do need to stay on top of a few things at once. This list of ingredients may look long, but I promise this is simple to make. I'll talk you through it. If you want to do this really quickly or are feeling very lazy, you could use a massaman curry paste—bigger supermarkets stock good ones. I always take the extra few minutes to make the paste, though. You can also make a double batch of the paste and freeze some. If you can't get unsalted peanuts, roasted salted ones will do. I rinse them with cold water and drain on paper towels so it's not a salt overload.

Fill and boil a kettle of water and get all your ingredients and equipment together. You'll need a small food processor or blender for the paste, a couple of large saucepans, and a frying pan.

Keeping the skins on, chop the potatoes into ½- to 1-inch/1- to 2-cm chunks. Put them into a pan, cover with boiling water, add some salt, then bring to a boil and cook until tender—this should take about 5 minutes.

Put your brown rice into another pan with twice its volume of cold water, some salt, and a dollop of coconut oil and put over high heat to boil for

**SERVES 4**

**FOR THE PASTE**

½ teaspoon fennel seeds

½ teaspoon coriander seeds

seeds from 6 cardamom pods

½ teaspoon black peppercorns

½ teaspoon ground cloves

½ teaspoon ground turmeric

½ teaspoon ground cinnamon

½ teaspoon dried chile flakes

a thumb-size piece of ginger

1 shallot

1 stalk of lemongrass

a large bunch of cilantro

2 cloves garlic

coconut oil

**FOR THE CURRY**

17 ounces/500 g new potatoes

sea salt

5 ounces/150 g unsalted peanuts

1 (14-ounce/400-g) can of coconut milk

2 tablespoons tamarind paste

1 tablespoon runny honey

7 ounces/200 g green beans, trimmed

7 ounces/200 g firm tofu

2 slices of fresh pineapple

INGREDIENTS CONTINUED →

CONTINUED

THE REST

¾ cup/150 g brown basmati rice

coconut oil

2 medium carrots

1 lime

a squeeze of runny honey

a splash of rice wine vinegar

sea salt

5 ounces/150 g kale,
stems removed and chopped

freshly ground pepper

1¾ ounces/50 g mixed toasted
seeds (I use a mixture of poppy,
sesame, and pumpkin)

20 to 25 minutes. Keep an eye on the rice while you do your other jobs, making sure it doesn't boil dry.

Next, make the paste. Toast the fennel, coriander, cardamom, and peppercorns in a dry pan for a couple of minutes, then put into a food processor with all the other ground spices and the chile flakes. Coarsely chop the peeled ginger and shallot, discard the tough outer layer of the lemongrass and chop the inner stalk, then add it all to the processor. Cut the stalks off the cilantro and add these with the garlic. Add a couple of tablespoons of coconut oil and blend on high until you have a paste.

Heat a large pan over high heat, then add the peanuts and stir for a minute before adding the paste. Fry for a couple of minutes more, then add the coconut milk, tamarind, honey, and a good pinch of salt. Drain the potatoes, add them to the sauce, and cook for 5 to 10 minutes, until it's a good consistency.

To make the quick pickle, grate the carrots into a bowl and add the zest and juice of a lime, a squeeze of honey, a splash of vinegar, and a pinch of salt. Finely chop the cilantro leaves and add to the bowl, then put to one side.

Use the pan you toasted the spices in to pan-fry the kale over medium heat in a little coconut oil, adding some salt and black pepper, until wilted but starting to crisp.

Once the potatoes have had 5 minutes in the sauce, add the green beans. Cut the tofu into ¾-inch/2-cm lengths, then cut the pineapple into pieces about the same size, discarding the skin. Add both to the curry and simmer for a few minutes, topping up with hot water if the curry is getting dry.

Once the rice and the curry are ready, ladle the rice into bowls and top generously with the curry. Finish off with a pinch of carrot pickle, some kale, and a sprinkling of seeds.

# Smoky root vegetable tacos with green chile salsa

SERVES 4

3 medium beets
(about 9 ounces/250 g)

2 sweet potatoes
(about 17 ounces/500 g)

sea salt

3 tablespoons coconut oil

½ bunch of green onions

2 carrots

a small bunch of radishes

2 unwaxed limes

sea salt

2 ripe avocados

1 teaspoon chipotle paste,
or 1 chopped red chile

1 teaspoon smoked paprika

a tiny squeeze of runny honey

freshly ground pepper

8 corn tortillas

FOR THE SALSA

2 tomatoes

1 tablespoon chipotle paste

1 green chile

1 tablespoon maple syrup

1 tablespoon red wine vinegar

a small bunch of cilantro

sea salt and freshly ground pepper

I like everything about tacos. The way they get scooped up in hands, the way they layer flavor and texture, and the way you can put bowls of each brightly colored filling in the middle of the table for everyone to help themselves and make their tacos their way.

I make tacos a lot at home, so I have been experimenting with lots of flavors. I wanted a version that was flavor-packed but super quick and easy. So these are a happy marriage of chipotle, crispy root vegetables, sweet onions, pickled cabbage, and a spicy green-chile-and-cilantro-spiked sauce.

I use 100 percent corn tortillas here—I buy them online in big batches and freeze them until they are needed. You can buy authentic tortillas in most supermarkets and Latino markets. If you prefer, regular flour tortillas (the smallest ones you can find) stand in nicely.

.........................................................................................

Fill and boil a kettle of water and get all your ingredients together.

Peel the beets and, using a sharp knife or a mandoline, slice them as thinly as possible. Chop the sweet potatoes into ¾-inch/2-cm chunks. Put the sweet potato into a small saucepan. Cover with boiling water, add a pinch of salt, and put over high heat. Bring to a boil, then simmer for 10 minutes, until soft.

Put a large frying pan over high heat and add 2 tablespoons of coconut oil. Slice the green onions as finely as you can, then add to the pan and sauté for 2–3 minutes, until beginning to brown. Remove from the pan and keep to one side. Add the beet slices to the pan and fry until crisp. You might need to do this in batches, depending on the size of your pan. Keep a close eye on them as they will brown quickly. Remove from the pan, and drain on some paper towels.

CONTINUED

Meanwhile, make the salsa. Put the tomatoes, chipotle paste, green chile, maple syrup, and vinegar into a blender with a good pinch of salt and the stalks from the bunch of cilantro. Blend until you have a spoonable, pretty smooth salsa. Season well with salt and pepper and set aside.

Using a vegetable peeler, peel the carrots and radishes into strips, then put them into a bowl with the zest and juice of a lime and a good pinch of salt and mix well.

Cut the avocados in half and pop out the pits. Using a knife, slice the halves finely all the way to the skin, then use a spoon to scoop out the sliced flesh.

Drain the sweet potatoes and put them back into the pan. Chop the cilantro leaves and add to the pan with the chipotle paste or chopped red chile, smoked paprika, honey, cooked green onions, and a good pinch of salt and pepper.

Warm the tortillas by holding each one over a flame for a few seconds on each side (if you don't have a gas stove you can warm them in a hot pan).

When you are ready to eat, spread equal amounts of the sweet potatoes over each tortilla and, top with the carrot and radish, crispy beets, some avocado, and a little of the salsa.

# Parsnip and potato rösti

There is something clean and Alpine about a *rösti* (potato pancake), while at the same time it is super-satisfying. Using parsnips in a *rösti* adds a sweetness and savoriness that a potato *rösti* doesn't have. Here the *rösti* is served with grilled leeks and lemony greens, with the option to add a little ricotta.

Preheat the oven to 425°F/220°C (convection 400°F/200°C) and get all your ingredients together. Heat a grill pan over high heat.

Beat two eggs together. Peel the parsnips and potatoes and coarsely grate them into a mixing bowl. Squeeze the grated vegetables in your hands or in a clean kitchen towel to get rid of most of the moisture, then put back into the bowl and add the beaten eggs and the thyme leaves. Season with salt and pepper and mix well.

Heat an ovenproof shallow casserole or frying pan, then add a good drizzle of oil and the parsnip mixture. Pat out to form a thick rösti and cook over high heat for a couple of minutes, then put into the oven and roast for 20 minutes.

Grill the leeks until charred on all sides, and then put into the oven to keep warm with the rösti. Wilt the spinach in a frying pan with a little olive oil, then take off the heat, season well with sea salt and pepper, and grate over the zest of the lemon.

A couple of minutes before your rösti is ready, fry the eggs in a little ghee. Once the rösti has had its time, take out the leeks and mix them with the spinach. Pile this and the ricotta, if using, on top of the rösti. Serve with fried eggs.

SERVES 4 TO 6

FOR THE RÖSTI
2 free-range or organic eggs
1⅓ pounds/600 g parsnips (4 to 6)
2 large potatoes
leaves from a small bunch of thyme
sea salt and freshly ground pepper
olive oil

FOR THE TOPPING
5 ounces/150 g baby leeks
7 ounces/200 g spinach
olive oil
sea salt and freshly ground pepper
1 unwaxed lemon

TO SERVE (OPTIONAL)
6 free-range or organic eggs
ghee
3½ ounces/100 g ricotta cheese

# Fragrant herb and star anise pho

I love the idea of *pho*: noodles, herbs, and a soothing broth. But most *pho* is made with a bone broth. Some places make a vegetarian version, but I have to say I have never had a good one, so I've always felt a bit left out of the *pho* craze. Well, this is a killer vegetarian version. The key here is charring the onions and garlic well first, which gives a rich, smoky flavor to the stock. I have made this for a number of *pho* connoisseurs and it got the seal of approval.

I often make double the amount of stock in my biggest pan and freeze half to use as a really full-flavored addition to soups and stews. You can use normal basil here, but if you are lucky enough to be able to get your hands on them, you could also use shiso and Vietnamese mint and basil.

If you are really hungry, then some pan-fried tofu, tossed in maple and soy at the end of cooking, would be a good addition.

....................................................................................................

Fill and boil a kettle of water and get all your ingredients together. Heat a large saucepan over high heat.

Quarter the onions, halve the head of garlic, and bash the ginger until it almost starts to break up. Add the onion, ginger, and garlic to the dry pan and toast until blackened and charred all over. This will take 4 to 5 minutes.

Next, add the cinnamon, star anise, cloves, and coriander seeds and toast for a couple of minutes, until they smell amazing, stirring all the time. Now add 2 quarts/2 liters of hot water from the kettle, the stock powder, the mushrooms, and the soy or tamari and bring to a simmer. Chop the carrots into ¾-inch/2-cm chunks and add these too. Cook for 25 minutes, until all the flavors have infused.

While the stock is simmering, refill and boil the kettle. Put the noodles into

⋮ CONTINUED

## SERVES 4

### FOR THE STOCK

2 onions

1 head of garlic

a small hand of ginger

2-inch/5-cm cinnamon stick

4 star anise

3 cloves

1 tablespoon coriander seeds

1 teaspoon vegetable stock powder or ½ stock cube

a large handful of dried mushrooms (Asian if you can find them)

1 tablespoon soy sauce or tamari

4 carrots

### FOR THE REST

7 ounces/200 g dried flat rice noodles or pho noodles

a small bunch of Thai or Vietnamese basil or other herbs

a small bunch of cilantro

10 ounces/300 g bok choy or spinach

7 ounces/200 g sugar snap peas

4 or 5 limes

7 ounces/200 g bean sprouts

chile oil

a bowl, cover with boiling water, and put to one side, draining after 8 minutes or following the instructions on the package.

Pick the leaves from the stalks of all your herbs, quarter your bok choy, and halve your sugar snap peas lengthwise.

Once the stock has had its time, sieve it into a large bowl and pour it back into the pan. Add the juice of 3 to 4 limes, depending on how juicy they are. Taste and adjust, making sure the lime, soy, and spices come through (I usually add another tablespoon of soy here), then add the sugar snap peas and bok choy and simmer for a couple of minutes, until the leaves have wilted a little.

Divide the drained noodles between four bowls and ladle over the stock and vegetables. Serve with bean sprouts and herbs and the remaining lime, cut into wedges, with some chile oil for everyone to add as they choose.

# Mung bean dal

Mung bean dal has long been one of my favorite things to eat when I feel in need of some goodness. It is used in the ayurvedic tradition to nourish and calm the body. Mung beans are naturally high in protein, so they are an amazing thing to include in a plant-based diet. You can find mung beans in all big supermarkets, health food shops, and Indian shops. They are little green beans—don't confuse them with mung dal, which are split yellow lentils.

Try to soak your mung beans overnight if you can, as they will cook quicker and be easier to digest. This is a great recipe for doubling up, to freeze in portions for days when nourishment needs to be really quick and easy.

I eat this with some coconut yogurt and a spoonful of mango or cilantro chutney (see page 183 for a good quick mango pickle).

**SERVES 6**

1 leek or onion

2 cloves garlic

a thumb-size piece of ginger

1 tablespoon coconut oil

1 teaspoon mustard seeds

2 teaspoons cumin seeds

17 ounces/500 g mung beans (ideally soaked overnight in cold water)

1 tablespoon vegetable stock powder or 1 stock cube

½ teaspoon ground turmeric

1 teaspoon ground cinnamon

1 medium tomato

2 medium hot chiles

a bunch of fresh cilantro

sea salt

1 tablespoon lemon juice, or to taste

1 large handful of spinach per person

Fill and boil a kettle of water and get all your ingredients together.

Wash and finely chop the leek or chop the onion, finely slice the garlic, and peel and coarsely chop the ginger. Heat the coconut oil in a pan over medium heat, add the mustard seeds and cumin seeds, and fry until they start to pop, then add the leek or onion, ginger, and garlic and cook for 8 to 10 minutes, or until soft and sweet.

Add the rinsed and drained mung beans with 1 quart/1 liter of boiling water from the kettle and the stock powder. Add the turmeric and cinnamon, then bring to a medium simmer.

Coarsely chop the tomato and finely chop the chiles (taking the seeds out if they're really hot ones). Finely chop the cilantro stalks. Add all these to the pan of mung beans, and simmer for 40 minutes.

Once the mung beans are tender, stir well, season well with sea salt, and squeeze in the lemon juice. Stir in the cilantro leaves and spinach.

# 5 one-pan dinners

I love any dinner that's made in one baking dish—less messing around, less washing up, and nothing to do while it all bakes. Here are some of my favorites, but you can freestyle as long as you mix a couple of vegetables, a bit of liquid (or a vegetable that will release some liquid), an herb, and something hearty like beans or torn-up bread. Use a deep, approximately 9 by 11-inch/23 by 28-cm baking dish here. Each serves 4.

### CRISPY RED PEPPER AND CANNELLINI BAKE

· 4 sliced peppers
· 2 handfuls of cherry tomatoes
· a small bunch of thyme
· 14-ounce/400-g can or 1⅓ cups/250 g cooked cannellini beans
· bread crumbs to top

●

bake for 40 minutes at 425°F/220°C (convection 400°F/200°C)

### HERBED WINTER ROOT GRATIN

· 1¾ pounds/800 g winter root vegetables, chopped
· a bunch of sage, thyme, or rosemary
· 2 torn-up slices of bread
· ½ cup/100 ml vegetable stock
· olive oil
· orange zest

●

bake for 50 minutes at 425°F/220°C (convection 400°F/200°C)

### ZUCCHINI, LEMON, AND LIMA BEAN BAKE

- 4 zucchini, sliced
- 7 ounces/200 g spinach
- 14-ounce/400-g can of lima beans
- zest of 1 lemon
- ½ cup/100 ml vegetable stock
- basil to finish

•

bake for 30 minutes at
425°F/220°C (convection 400°F/200°C)

### SQUASH, PAPRIKA, AND CHICKPEA BAKE

- 1 coarsely chopped winter squash
- 14-ounce/400-g can of chickpeas
- pinch of smoked paprika
- ½ jar of roasted red peppers
- ½ cup/100 ml vegetable stock
- 1 chopped red chile

•

bake for 50 minutes at
425°F/220°C (convection 400°F/200°C)

### BAKED SWEET POTATO RÖSTI

- 1⅓ pounds/600 g grated sweet potatoes
- Dijon mustard
- spinach
- peas
- lemon zest

•

bake for 40 minutes at
425°F/220°C (convection 400°F/200°C),
top with poached eggs

# Celery root, bay leaf, and mushroom ragù

This is my kind of comfort food, unfussy and warming but naturally rich and amazingly tasty. This is deep, wintry, woody food for cold nights under blankets with the fire going. It also makes a brilliant pie or tart filling.

I eat this with mashed root vegetables or quick polenta, depending on what I've got in the cupboard. I use cider here, as I like its sweet notes alongside the celery root, but white wine would work just as well.

If I can get my hands on them, I use wild mushrooms, but chestnut or some of the more exotic mushrooms would be great too.

..................................................................................................

Fill and boil a kettle of water and get all your ingredients together. Heat a large Dutch oven over high heat.

Chop the leek and onion and add these to the pot with a glug of olive oil, stirring from time to time while you coarsely chop the carrot and celery. Add these to the pan too and cook for 5 minutes, stirring, while you get on with some more chopping.

Heat a large frying pan over high heat. Chop the mushrooms, or tear them into bite-sized pieces, then add to the frying pan with a little olive oil and allow to cook for a couple of minutes. Chop the garlic and add to the pan when the mushrooms are nearly ready. You want the mushrooms to be starting to brown and crisp around the edges.

Peel and chop the celery root into roughly ¾-inch/2-cm pieces. Once the vegetables in the pot have had 5 minutes, add the herbs along with the mushrooms and chopped celery root and cook for a couple of minutes. Add the peppercorns, cider, Worcestershire sauce, and stock and bring to a boil, then simmer for 20 to 30 minutes until you have a thick, rich sauce.

SERVES 4 TO 6

1 leek

1 red onion

olive oil

1 large carrot

2 celery stalks

9 ounces/250 g mixed mushrooms

4 cloves garlic

1 medium celery root
(about 1¾ pounds/800 g)

a couple of sprigs of sage

a couple of bay leaves

a few sprigs of thyme

20 black peppercorns

1¼ cups/300 ml good cider

2 tablespoons vegetarian Worcestershire sauce

1 tablespoon low-salt vegetable stock powder or ½ low-salt stock cube

FOR THE HERB OIL

a small bunch of thyme or rosemary

4 tablespoons extra-virgin olive oil

TO SERVE

mashed potatoes or cooked polenta

a few tablespoons of crème fraîche (optional)

mustard or horseradish (optional)

40 MINUTES

Now get on with whatever you are going to serve this with—I favor polenta or mashed sweet potatoes. But regular mashed potatoes work perfectly too.

To make your herb oil, put all the herbs into a blender with a drizzle of the oil and blend, adding more oil, until you have a grassy green paste.

Once the ragù is ready, spoon it into a bowl on top of a pile of polenta or mashed potatoes and drizzle over the herb oil. Add a little crème fraîche and mustard or horseradish, if you like. Winter in a bowl.

# Turkish flatbreads with spoon salad

SERVES 4

**FOR THE FLATBREADS**

1⅔ cups/200 g spelt flour, plus extra for dusting

1 teaspoon baking powder

¾ cup/200 g Greek yogurt, or ⅔ cup/150 ml warm water

**FOR THE TOPPING**

2 red onions

3 red bell peppers

2 tablespoons olive oil

1 teaspoon dried Turkish chile flakes (see headnote)

1 green chile

a small bunch of mint

**FOR THE SALAD**

1 red onion

1 lemon

sea salt

5 vine-ripe tomatoes

a small bunch of mint

a small bunch of parsley

freshly ground pepper

1 tablespoon sumac

1 teaspoon harissa or Turkish chile paste

2 tablespoons pomegranate molasses

extra-virgin olive oil

The part of East London I live in is full of Turkish cafés. They turn out charcoal-baked flatbreads and insanely good salads, and although meat is front and center in Turkish food, there are some amazing vegetable dishes too.

Here is a quick way to make my two favorites at home. Amazing, fluffy, quick Turkish flatbreads from the frying pan, topped with caramelized onions and smoky red peppers, and my favorite-ever salad—sometimes called ezme salad, but I prefer its other name: spoon salad.

I use Turkish chile here, which has a milder flavor, somewhere between a chile and a red bell pepper, but if you can't get your hands on it, you can use regular dried chile flakes, but more sparingly. Similarly, if you can't get pomegranate molasses, a 50:50 mixture of good balsamic and honey will do.

These flatbreads are brilliantly flavor-packed as they are, but sometimes to mix things up I add some crumbled feta on top. If you are in a hurry, this topping can be used to top ready-made pitas or flatbreads, which will save a lot of time.

.................................................................

Get all your ingredients together.

Put all the flatbread ingredients into the bowl of your food processor and pulse until the mixture forms a ball. If you don't have a food processor, this can be done in a bowl using a fork to begin with, followed by your hands, but it will take a little longer.

Dust a clean work surface with flour and tip out the dough. Knead for a minute or so to bring it all together. This is a quick flatbread recipe, so you don't need to knead it for long. Put the dough into a flour-dusted bowl and

⫶⟩ CONTINUED

cover with a plate. Put to one side to rise a little for 10 to 15 minutes while you do some other jobs. Don't expect it to rise like normal dough, but it may puff up a tiny bit.

To make the topping, heat a frying pan over medium heat, then finely chop your onions and red peppers and put them into the pan with 1 tablespoon of oil. Cook over medium heat for 10 minutes, until soft and sweet, then add the dried chile. Chop the fresh green chile and mint and add to the pan along with a final tablespoon of oil. Stir, then take off the heat and season well.

Next, make your salad. Finely slice the onion and put into a bowl with the juice of half a lemon and a good pinch of salt. Scrunch with your hands, then leave to pickle.

Chop the tomatoes coarsely, then coarsely chop the leaves of the fresh mint and parsley. Put them into a bowl with the pepper, sumac, harissa, and the pomegranate molasses and add the lemon-pickled red onions. Season well with salt and pepper and add a little more lemon juice and a good drizzle of olive oil, balancing out the flavors until it tastes great.

Now back to the flatbreads. Put a large frying pan or grill pan (about 9 inches/22 to 24 cm) over medium heat.

Dust a clean work surface and rolling pin with flour, then divide the dough into four equal-sized pieces. Using your hands, pat and flatten out the dough, then use the rolling pin to roll each piece into about an 8-inch/20-cm round, roughly ⅛ inch/2 to 3 mm thick.

Once your pan is hot, cook each flatbread for 1 to 2 minutes on each side, until nicely puffed up, turning with tongs.

Spread with the onion and chile mixture while hot, and serve right away with spoonfuls of salad.

# Supper samosas with quick mango pickle

Samosas are always seen as a snack, and are often deep-fried and full of what I call school-lunch vegetables: carrots, peas, potatoes. Good as they are that way, these are a little different—fresher, cleaner, and oven-baked. I make them into the main event of my dinner and pair them with a quick homemade mango pickle.

The folding can take a bit of practice. If you get stuck, there are some brilliant videos online that might help you out. Serve this, if you like, with a quick salad of grated carrot and cilantro.

Preheat the oven to 425°F/220°C (convection 400°F/200°C) and get all your ingredients together.

Pulse the cauliflower in a food processor until you have ricelike shards.

Finely chop the green onions and put them into a pan with a little coconut oil or ghee. Fry for a couple of minutes, until beginning to brown. Add the chopped chile and garlic, then the spices and curry leaves, and cook for another 2 minutes. Add the cauliflower, spinach, chopped cilantro, a squeeze of lemon, and a good pinch of salt and cook for 5 minutes, then lay the mixture on a tray to cool down quickly.

Melt 4 tablespoons of coconut oil or ghee and have this ready along with a pastry brush. Remove your filo pastry from the package and keep under a damp cloth or tea towel to stop it from drying out.

Lay one sheet of the pastry on a clean, dry work surface and cut it lengthwise into three long equal pieces. Put a heaped teaspoon of the cauliflower mixture on the bottom left of the pastry, then fold the right-hand corner over the mixture; this will create a triangle shape. Continue the folding, keeping the

 CONTINUED

SERVES 6
(MAKES 24 SAMOSAS)

14 ounces/400 g cauliflower
4 green onions
coconut oil or ghee
1 green chile
2 cloves garlic
1 teaspoon cumin seeds
1 teaspoon mustard seeds
1 teaspoon garam masala
a small handful of curry leaves
2 big handfuls of spinach
a bunch of cilantro
1 lemon
sea salt
8 to 10 ounces/250 to 300 g filo pastry (12 sheets)
nigella seeds

FOR THE MANGO PICKLE
2 ripe mangoes
1 teaspoon nigella seeds
a pinch of fennel seeds
a pinch of mustard seeds
1 clove garlic
zest and juice of 1 unwaxed lime
1 tablespoon white wine vinegar

triangle shape, brushing a little oil in between each fold. You should then have a nicely triangular-shaped samosa. Give it a final brush with oil and sprinkle with the nigella seeds. Repeat with the rest of the pastry and the mixture. Bake in the oven for 15 minutes.

Meanwhile, make a quick mango chutney. With the skin still on, cut off the cheeks of each mango, leaving the pit behind. Carefully slice into the cheek, almost all the way into the skin, in $\frac{1}{2}$-inch/1-cm strips, and then across to make $\frac{1}{2}$-inch/1-cm squares. Push from the skin side to flip the mango into a hedgehog, and use a spoon to scrape off the roughly $\frac{1}{2}$-inch/1-cm pieces of flesh. In a small saucepan, toast the spices, then add the mango and lime juice and vinegar. Cook for 5 minutes until the mango has started to break down, then take off the heat. Serve the samosas with the pickle.

# Roasted vegetables, grapes, and lentils

This is a dinner I ate one January day when staying with my sister in Silver Lake. L.A. is never cold, but it can get cold enough to make you crave something substantial, and this is filling and hearty even if you don't have to crawl under a blanket on the sofa. It's perfect for cooler nights, when the winter cravings for bowls of mashed potatoes and peas have passed.

I try to get my hands on smaller sweet potatoes—they are somehow sweeter and bake whole quicker—but if you can't get them, big ones cut into quarters will do just fine.

I use interesting smaller squashes here, like the vivid reddish-orange red kuri, the deep green and aptly shaped acorn, and the frilly-when-cut delicata, which all work well, but a standard butternut will do the trick too.

SERVES 6

FOR THE ROASTED VEGETABLES

4 small sweet potatoes

olive oil

sea salt

2 small winter squashes

1 small butternut squash

1 small cauliflower

freshly ground pepper

a large bunch of grapes

leaves from a small bunch of sage

leaves from a small bunch of thyme

juice of 1 lemon

FOR THE LENTILS

14 ounces/400 g Puy lentils, washed

4 cloves garlic, unpeeled

1 small tomato

1 bay leaf

1 quart/1 liter vegetable stock

Preheat the oven to 425°F/220°C (convection 400°F/200°C). Fill and boil a kettle of water and get all your ingredients together.

Rub the sweet potatoes with a little olive oil and sprinkle with salt, then place on a baking sheet and roast in the oven for 40 to 45 minutes, until soft.

Cut the squash into ½-inch/1-cm slices and break the cauliflower into small florets. Place them both on another baking sheet with a good pinch of salt and pepper and a drizzle of olive oil, toss to coat, and roast for about 40 minutes or so.

Meanwhile, cook the lentils. Put them into a pan with the unpeeled garlic, whole tomato, and bay leaf. Just cover with vegetable stock, place over medium heat, bring to a simmer, and let them simmer away for 20 to 25 minutes, until the lentils are cooked and the water has evaporated. If they are looking too dry, top up with a little boiling water as needed.

CONTINUED

Once the lentils are cooked, take the garlic and tomato out of the pan. Pop the garlic cloves out of their skins, mash with the tomato and a couple of spoonfuls of the lentils, then stir back into the pan with a couple of spoonfuls of olive oil. The lentils should become nice and creamy.

When there is 10 minutes' cooking time left on the squash and sweet potatoes, put the grapes on a baking tray, breaking them up a little. Scatter over the sage and thyme leaves, drizzle with olive oil, and roast for 5 to 10 minutes, until the grapes are sweet and sticky.

Once the grapes are cooked, take them out of the oven and pour the liquid from the tray into a bowl. Add a good glug of olive oil, the lemon juice, and some salt and pepper. Tumble all the vegetables and the grapes onto a platter and dress with the grape dressing, put the lentils into a big bowl, and serve both in the middle of the table.

# Charred celery root steaks
# with crispy sweet potato fries

SERVES 2

2 sweet potatoes

canola or olive oil

sea salt and freshly ground pepper

1 tablespoon polenta

3 cloves garlic

1 celery root

1 ounce/25 g Parmesan cheese
(I use a vegetarian one)

FOR THE MARINADE

1 red chile

zest and juice of 1 unwaxed lemon

1 tablespoon maple syrup

leaves of a few sprigs of thyme

sea salt and freshly ground pepper

FOR THE SALSA VERDE

3 cornichons

1 tablespoon capers

1 small bunch each of mint,
basil, and parsley

zest and juice of
½ unwaxed lemon

2 tablespoons extra-virgin olive oil

sea salt and freshly ground pepper

green salad, to serve (optional)

Celery root is a brute of a vegetable, but beneath its gnarly, knobbly exterior lies sweet creamy white flesh that I adore. Celery root takes on flavor brilliantly and can stand up to some brave flavors and cooking. Here it's marinated, charred on a grill pan, and basted with chile and thyme to create a burnished crust.

Salsa verde always reminds me of my days in the kitchen—it was one of the first things I learned to make as a chef and it's still one of my favorites. It cuts through the sweet smokiness of the celery root perfectly.

These sweet potatoes are my favorite way to eat fries. Polenta-coated and oven-baked, they are crispy and perfect. If you can't get hold of polenta, another way to ensure really crisp fries without a lot of oil is to place a cooling rack on top of a baking sheet and bake the fries on the rack.

This is also a great thing to do on the barbecue—the fries won't take the high heat, but the celery root steaks will be all the better for some smoky flames.

.................................................................................................................

Preheat the oven to 400°F/200°C (convection 375°F/180°C). Fill and boil a kettle of water and get all your ingredients together.

Carefully cut the sweet potatoes into thin sticks about ½ inch/1 cm thick. Place them on a rimmed baking sheet, drizzle with the oil, season with salt and pepper, and scatter over the polenta. Crush the garlic cloves with the side of a knife, add them to the sheet, toss the whole lot to coat, and put into the oven for 25 minutes.

⁙ CONTINUED

Fill a medium saucepan with hot water from the kettle and bring to a
boil. Thickly peel the celery root, then slice it into ¾-inch/2-cm-thick
steaks and blanch in the boiling water for 5 minutes, until just tender.

To make the marinade, finely chop the red chile and mix it with the lemon
zest and juice, maple syrup, thyme leaves, and a pinch each of salt and pepper.

Once the 5 minutes are up, drain the celery root and put it into the marinade.
Preheat a ridged grill pan over high heat. Remember to keep an eye on your
sweet potatoes and turn them from time to time so that they brown evenly.

To make the salsa verde, coarsely chop the cornichons and capers, then
add the herbs, and chop everything together. Scoop into a bowl, grate in
the lemon zest, squeeze in the juice, and add the oil and 2 tablespoons
of the marinade from the celery root. Taste and season with salt and pepper.

Place the celery root on the hot grill pan. Cook for 2 to 3 minutes on
each side, until charred and cooked through, basting with the remaining
marinade every minute or so.

Five minutes before the sweet potatoes are ready, turn the oven up to its
maximum temperature. Take the fries out, grate over the Parmesan, then
pop back into the oven to crisp up.

Serve the steaks with the fries and a generous spoon of salsa verde, and,
if you like, with a shock of green salad.

# Quick-pickled roasted root vegetables, polenta, and carrot-top pesto

This is my new favorite thing to cook when people come round for dinner. It's quick and satisfying but also elegant, super delicious, and surprising.

I'm going to show you a couple of ways to add flavor and create interesting nuances and layers that might be new to you. First, I quickly pickle the vegetables before they are roasted, giving them a delicious piquant note, which is balanced by a little honey. To top it off, I make a pesto of carrot tops, which taste a bit like parsley but are even more grassy and savory—they are delicious, and it's so satisfying to know that they have not been thrown away either by me or by the supermarket. If you can't find carrots with tops, a bunch of parsley will do in their place.

....................................................................................................................

Preheat the oven to 425°F/220°C (convection 400°F/200°C). Fill and boil a kettle of water and get all your ingredients together.

First, pickle your vegetables. Using a mandoline or your excellent knife skills, peel and finely slice the carrots (saving the tops for later) and beets and put them into a large bowl. Squeeze over the juice of 1½ lemons and add the red wine vinegar and honey. Add a couple of pinches each of salt and pepper and put to one side.

Now pour 6 cups/1.5 liters of boiling water into a large saucepan and bring to a simmer over medium heat. Slowly pour in the polenta, whisking as you go. Add a good pinch each of salt and pepper and continue to whisk as the mixture thickens. Add 3 tablespoons of olive oil and whisk it in, then leave on a very low heat to bubble away, whisking again from time to time. It will take about 25 minutes to cook.

∴ CONTINUED

## SERVES 4

4 carrots with tops (see headnote)

4 beets

2 lemons

1 tablespoon red wine vinegar

1 tablespoon runny honey

sea salt and freshly ground pepper

1⅔ cups/250 g polenta

extra-virgin olive oil

a small bunch of sage

a grating of Parmesan or pecorino cheese (I use a vegetarian one) (optional)

While this is happening, spread your pickled vegetables out over two baking rimmed baking sheet, drizzle with a little oil, and put into the oven to roast for 20 minutes. Reserve the pickling liquor for later.

Keep an eye on the polenta while you make a quick pesto with the carrot tops. Wash the carrot tops well and pat them dry. Pulse them in a food processor with the juice of the other lemon half, 3 tablespoons of olive oil, 3 tablespoons of the pickling liquor, and a good pinch each of salt and pepper.

Turn the vegetables in the oven—they should be starting to brown—and keep stirring the polenta. Pick the sage leaves from the stalks and toss them in a little olive oil.

Once the vegetables have had 20 minutes, scatter over the sage leaves, and put back into the oven for a further 5 minutes.

The polenta is cooked when you can no longer feel the grain—check by tasting a little, but let it cool down on the spoon first, as it will be very hot. Once it is ready, season well with salt and pepper and, if you are using it, grate in the cheese.

Serve the polenta topped with the roasted vegetables and the sage, and spoonfuls of the carrot-top pesto.

# Lentil ragù agrodolce

This is my version of spaghetti bolognese. This ragù has a real depth of flavor and the wonderful piquancy that *agrodolce* cooking is all about. I love this with regular pasta or zucchini noodles (see page 90) or even the chickpea pasta on page 196. I switch among them to suit my mood and the season.

This keeps in the fridge for four days and freezes really well. I freeze it in portion-sized batches for super-quick weeknight dinners. Leftovers are also particularly good on top of a baked potato or roasted sweet potato.

Fill and boil a kettle of water and get all your ingredients together.

Peel the carrots and cut them into fine dice, then put them into a heavy pan with the oil. Cook over medium heat while you finely chop the onion, then add this to the pan and cook for another 10 minutes, or until the onion is soft, sweet, and nicely browned.

Add the lentils, then pour in the passata and the vegetable stock powder with half a can of hot water from the kettle. Coarsely chop the dates and the chile and add to the pan with the vinegar. Simmer for 25 minutes until you have a thick, rich ragù.

Put a large pan of water on to boil for the pasta and salt it generously. Once the lentils have had 25 minutes, cook the pasta and drain, reserving a cup or so of the cooking water.

When the lentil ragù is ready, take off the heat and mash half with a potato masher, then return to the heat for a couple of minutes.

Once the sauce is ready, add the drained pasta and a cup of pasta water if needed. Serve with Parmesan.

### SERVES 4

2 carrots

3 tablespoons olive oil

1 onion

1 (14-ounce/400-g) can of Puy lentils, or 1¼ cups/250 g home-cooked lentils (see pages 241–245)

1½ cups/350 ml passata (see page 117)

1 teaspoon vegetable stock powder or ½ stock cube

2 medjool dates, pitted

1 red chile, seeded

2 tablespoons balsamic vinegar

10 ounces/300 g pasta of your choice (I use pappardelle)

### TO SERVE

Parmesan cheese
(I use a vegetarian one)

# Chickpea pasta with simple tomato sauce

For years I have been dabbling with different grains and gluten-free flours in pursuit of my Holy Grail: a bowl of satisfying but light pasta with bite and backbone that doesn't leave me needing a two-hour nap.

And I think I've cracked it. These super-simple noodles are made from chickpea flour and use flaxseeds to bind them. They are quick and easy to roll by hand, but if you have the time and inclination, a pasta machine would make them neatly perfect.

They are naturally vegan and gluten-free and are all the more interesting and delicious for it.

If you don't use flaxseed at home already and are worried that the remainder of the bag will lurk untouched at the back of the cupboard, don't be—flaxseed is incredibly good for you and is brilliant added to morning smoothies, porridge, cereals, and baking. It's one of the best plant-based sources of alpha-linolenic acid, which converts in the body to the same heart-protective, omega-3 fatty acids found in salmon, sardines, and mackerel. It also contains both soluble and insoluble fiber, which helps our intestines. In addition, flaxseed is one of the richest dietary sources of lignans, phytoestrogens thought to protect against cancer of the breast, prostate, and colon.

Fill and boil a kettle of water and get all your ingredients and equipment together.

Mix together the flaxseed and 2/3 cup/150 ml of warm water and leave it to sit for a couple of minutes until thickened. Put the flax mixture, chickpea flour, and 3/4 cup/180 ml of cold water into a food processor with 1 tablespoon of olive oil and a good pinch of salt, and pulse until it forms

⸭ CONTINUED

## SERVES 4

4 tablespoons ground flaxseed

3¾ cup/350 g chickpea flour, plus extra for dusting

olive oil

sea salt

### FOR THE SAUCE

2 cloves garlic

1 (14-ounce/400-g) can of chopped tomatoes

leaves from a big bunch of basil

### TO SERVE (OPTIONAL)

pecorino or Parmesan cheese (I use a vegetarian one)

a doughy ball. You can do this easily in a bowl by hand too. Wrap the ball of dough in a clean kitchen towel or plastic wrap and set aside for 10 minutes.

Heat a frying pan over high heat, then thinly slice the garlic and add it to the pan with a little olive oil. Fry for a minute or two, until the edges are beginning to brown. Quickly add the tomatoes and leave to simmer over medium heat for 10 minutes, until thickened and glossy. Fill a large pan with hot water from the kettle, add a good pinch of salt, and bring to a boil, ready for the pasta.

Unwrap your dough and cut it into two pieces. Flour your work surface generously with chickpea flour. Use a rolling pin to roll out the dough as thinly as you can, as it will expand a little as it cooks, then use a knife to cut the dough into ¼-inch/5-mm-wide ribbons. Place on a floured tray and repeat with the other half of the dough.

Once you have cut all your pasta, add it to the boiling water for 2 to 3 minutes—no longer or it will start to break up a bit. Don't worry if some of the pasta breaks a little; this pasta is more delicate than the regular sort. Using a slotted spoon, drain it and add it to the tomato sauce with most of the basil leaves. Toss gently to coat all the pasta, adding a little of the cooking water from the pan if it looks a bit thick.

Serve with a little more basil scattered over and some pecorino or Parmesan, if you like.

# Beet and radicchio gratin

This is a tray of crisp-edged beets, winter herbs, and golden potatoes. A plate of incredible tones of deep pink and purple—lurid colors, but soft, sweet, warming, and super tasty flavors. The beets perfectly counter the gentle bitterness of the radicchio, so if you are new to bitter leaves, this is a great place to start. If you can't find radicchio, a couple of purple endives will work well.

Bitter leaves are really good for digestion. They are even thought to help counter cravings for sweet foods, and if you are anything like me, sometimes a bit of help with the sugar cravings can be a good thing.

I top this gratin with a punchy gremolata—chopped fresh herbs with proud amounts of citrus and garlic; the grassy freshness, zippy orange, and punch of garlic take this gratin to the next level. I serve it with a watercress salad, but if you like, you could have some bread on the side for mopping up the juices.

........................................................................................................

Preheat the oven to 425°F/220°C (convection 400°F/200°C). Fill and boil a kettle of water and get all your ingredients and equipment together.

Peel the beets and use a food processor or a mandoline to finely slice them. Scatter them in a deep baking dish approximately 8 by 10 inches/ 20 by 25 cm. Slice the potatoes in the same way and scatter them over the beets. Shred the radicchio as you would a head of lettuce—avoiding and discarding the root—and add this to the baking dish too.

Pick the leaves off the stalks of the thyme and sage and slice the garlic, and add these to the dish, then grate over the zest of the lemon and season well with salt and pepper. Toss everything together, then use your hands

⠿ CONTINUED

## SERVES 4

1⅔ pounds/750 g beets

10 ounces/300 g small to medium waxy potatoes

1 head of radicchio

a few sprigs of thyme

a few sprigs of sage

3 cloves garlic

1 unwaxed lemon

sea salt and freshly ground pepper

½ cup/125 ml white wine

½ cup/125 ml hot vegetable stock

## FOR THE GREMOLATA

a small bunch of parsley

½ clove garlic

1 red chile

zest of 1 large unwaxed orange

watercress or arugula salad, to serve (optional)

bread, to serve (optional)

to press and push everything level in the dish. Pour over the white wine and the hot stock—the liquid should come about halfway up the potatoes—and bake for 30 minutes.

Meanwhile, make the gremolata. Finely chop the parsley, garlic, and chile and put into a bowl with the orange zest. Mix well, season with a little salt and pepper, and put to one side.

Once the gratin is browned on top and crisp around the edges, it should be ready; check by pulling a potato from the middle of the gratin and making sure it's cooked through. Serve topped with the gremolata alongside a watercress or arugula salad and, if you like, some bread.

# quick flavor boosts

| **HERB OIL** | **PESTO** | **HERB SMASH** |
|---|---|---|
| On top of soups, stews, dressings, grains, salads, flatbreads, tofu | On top of pasta, crostini, pizza, green vegetables, baked potatoes, new potatoes, soups, sandwiches, tomatoes | On top of soups, stews, flatbreads, bruschetta, stirred through vegetables, with roasted root vegetables |
| A bunch of soft herbs | A bunch of soft herbs | A bunch of soft herbs |
| or | + | + |
| ½ a bunch of hardy herbs | A small handful of nuts | Zest of 1 lemon, orange, or lime |
| + | + | + |
| ⅓ cup/100 ml extra-virgin olive oil | ½ clove garlic (optional) | ½ clove garlic |
| + | + | + |
| Sea salt | Sea salt | 1 red or green chile |
| + | ↓ | + |
| Lemon juice to taste | Bash in mortar and pestle or blend | Sea salt and pepper |
| ↓ | + | ↓ |
| Blend until you have an herby green paste | 2 tablespoons olive oil | Chop all this together until you have a rough herb smash |
| | + | |
| | Juice of 1 lemon | |
| | ↓ | |
| | Mix well | |

Cooking fast is all about adding and layering flavor quickly and cleverly. One of the ways to do this at home is to add an instant boost with a simple but flavor-packed dressing or herb oil. These boosters will take a couple of minutes to make and they transform a simple bowl of quinoa or a pan of steamed broccoli into a dinner to be proud of. These rough recipes make enough for a few bowls of grains or vegetables. I have left them quite casual so that you can adapt them to your mood and to what they'll be piled on top of.

## MISO AND MAPLE DRESSING

On top of noodles,
rice, roasted vegetables,
green vegetables, tomatoes,
sandwiches

1 tablespoon dark miso

+

1 tablespoon soy sauce

+

1 tablespoon maple syrup

+

1 tablespoon rice vinegar

or

lime juice

↓

Mix well

## TAHINI DRESSING

On top of soups,
stews, sandwiches,
flatbreads,
falafels, salads

2 tablespoons tahini

+

Zest and juice of 1 lemon

+

2 tablespoons olive oil

+

1 finely chopped shallot

or

½ clove garlic,
finely chopped

+

Sea salt and pepper

↓

Mix well

## HARISSA DRESSING

On top of halloumi,
hummus,
flatbreads, salads,
cheese, soups

6 chopped green onions,
fried until soft and sweet

+

1 tablespoon harissa

+

2 tablespoons olive oil

+

Juice of 1 lemon

+

Sea salt and pepper

↓

Mix well

# Avocado and zucchini fries

SERVES 4

**FOR THE FRIES**

4 large zucchini

2 tablespoons polenta

1 ounce/25 g Parmesan cheese
(I use a vegetarian one) (optional)

sea salt and freshly ground pepper

**FOR THE AVOCADO**

2 just-ripe avocados

3½ ounces/100 g bread crumbs
or fine oats

a pinch of dried chile flakes

sesame seeds

sea salt and freshly ground pepper

2 free-range or organic eggs

**FOR THE PEAS**

7 ounces/200 g frozen peas

a few sprigs of mint

sea salt and freshly ground pepper

**FOR THE QUICK
TOMATO KETCHUP**

1 tablespoon tomato purée

6 cherry tomatoes

a splash of vegetarian
Worcestershire sauce

a splash of Tabasco sauce

a dash of maple syrup

This is my new comfort dish. To me it has the homely childhood associations, but the flavors are much more sophisticated. If you haven't cooked avocado before, I understand your trepidation—I was skeptical at first too, but it is a revelation. Baking the avocado enhances its butteriness and its grassy-fresh character. I serve this with an amazing homemade instant ketchup and some simple mashed minty peas.

Use just-ripe avocados here, as the super-ripe ones won't work. This can be made easily with oats in place of bread crumbs if you prefer. I use a cooling rack and a little polenta to allow the fries to get really crispy in the oven; using a cooling rack means the air circulates all around the fries, helping them crisp up. If you don't have one that fits in your oven, that's okay, the fries just might take a little longer to crisp.

Preheat the oven to 425°F/220°C (convection 400°F/200°C). Fill and boil a kettle of water and get all your ingredients together.

Slice the zucchini into thin batons, avoiding the fluffy middle bits. Pop them onto a baking sheet and scatter the polenta over. Grate over the Parmesan, if using, then sprinkle with salt and pepper and toss on the sheet to make sure each fry is coated well. Transfer the fries to a wire rack that fits on top of the baking sheet and bake for 35 minutes.

Cut your avocados in half and remove the pits, then carefully scoop out the flesh or peel off the skin, keeping the halves intact.

Mix the bread crumbs or oats (if they are very big oats, you might want to pulse them in a food processor first) with the chile, sesame seeds, and a good pinch of salt and pepper and put on a plate. Crack the eggs into a deep plate or shallow bowl. Season and whisk with a fork.

Take the avocado pieces and lower them into the egg mixture, turning them carefully to coat. Then toss the fries in the bread crumbs so they are coated evenly. Put the avocados into the oven next to the fries and bake for 25 minutes.

Put the peas into a small pan and cover with boiling water. Boil for a couple of minutes while you finely chop the mint. Drain the peas, add the mint and a good pinch of salt and pepper, and mash them a little.

Meanwhile, check your avocados and fries, turning them carefully so they cook evenly.

Next, put all the ingredients for the ketchup into a jug and blend with a handheld blender until smooth. Season with salt and pepper, then taste and adjust, adding more sweetness or vinegar if needed.

Once the avocado is browned and the fries are crisp, take them out of the oven and serve with the warm, minty peas and generous spoonfuls of ketchup.

# Sweet potato and ricotta gnocchi with almond pesto

These gnocchi are my kind of comfort food—light but hearty little sweet potato and ricotta dumplings, tossed in a quick, sweet basil and oregano pesto. Hearty enough for a winter dinner in front of the fire but fresh enough in flavor for an incredible summer supper.

This recipe goes against the gnocchi rules I learned as a chef. We used to make gnocchi with almost no flour and super-dry baked potatoes; they were delicious but took some skill and a great deal of patience.

This is a foolproof gnocchi recipe that comes together relatively quickly. The addition of some flour means the gnocchi are much easier to handle if you haven't made them before, and they are still utterly delicious.

If you are vegan, leave out the ricotta and use 7 ounces/200 g more of sweet potatoes. The recipe can easily be made with a gluten-free flour, such as buckwheat flour, as in this case the slightly drying nature of gluten-free flours is a plus.

Any leftover, uncooked gnocchi will keep well in the fridge for 2 to 3 days.

...................................................................................................................

Fill and boil a kettle of water and get all your ingredients together.

Peel the sweet potatoes, cut them into 1¼-inch/3-cm pieces and steam them; this will take about 20 minutes.

Meanwhile, make your pesto. Put the herbs and nuts into a food processor with the zest and juice of the lemon and pulse until you have a grassy green paste, then add olive oil gradually until you have a spoonable pesto. If you want to loosen it without adding too much oil, you could add a tablespoon of water. Season well with salt and pepper.

CONTINUED

## SERVES 6 TO 8

1¾ pounds/800 g sweet potatoes
7 ounces/200 g ricotta cheese
2½ cups/300 g light spelt flour
1 free-range or organic egg yolk, beaten
a little butter
olive oil

### FOR THE PESTO
2 large bunches of basil
a small bunch of oregano
1¾ ounces/50 g blanched almonds
1 unwaxed lemon
extra-virgin olive oil
sea salt and freshly ground pepper

### TO SERVE
a good grating of pecorino or Parmesan cheese (I use a vegetarian one) (optional)

Put a large pan of boiling salted water over high heat. Drain the sweet potatoes, allow them to steam dry for a couple of minutes to get rid of as much moisture as possible, then mash them well with a potato masher or a potato ricer.

Fold the ricotta, flour, and beaten egg yolk into the sweet potatoes. Leave the mixture for 5 minutes; then, on a well-floured surface, working with a quarter of the dough at a time, roll each quarter into two long, fattish sausages about ¾ inch/2 cm in diameter. Leave for a further couple of minutes to firm up.

Cut the sausages into ¾-inch/2-cm pieces. Keep these to one side while you roll and cut the rest of the gnocchi. Drop them into the boiling water and cook until they rise to the top.

Meanwhile, warm six bowls. Once the gnocchi have risen to the surface, scoop them out of the pan into a big bowl, then stir the pesto through before dividing among four bowls with grating of Parmesan or pecorino, if you like.

# Frying pan squash and kale pie

This pie is a meeting of two amazing dinners I ate in the same week. One was a light, crisp feta-and-spinach spanakopita pie in a no-frills Greek café, not far from home. The other was a pizza topped with smashed squash, crispy kale, and black olives in a great pizza place a few minutes' walk from my house. I loved the flavors of the pizza so much I wanted to work them into something that was quick enough to make on a weeknight, and this is it.

This is a cheat's pie that uses a frying pan instead of a tart pan and is filled with super-quick grated and chopped vegetables. Serve with lemon-dressed green salad and, if you like, some chile sauce.

..........................................................................................................................................

Preheat your oven to 425°F/220°C (convection 400°F/200°C) and get all your ingredients together. You'll need a 9½-inch/24-cm oven proof frying pan.

Heat a saucepan over low heat while you finely chop your onions, then turn the heat up to medium, add a little coconut oil, and cook the onions for 5 minutes, until soft and sweet.

While the onions are cooking, peel and coarsely dice the squash. Add it to the onions along with the thyme leaves and cook for 5 to 10 minutes, until the mixture is dry.

Meanwhile, unwrap the sheets of filo and lay them over your frying pan, allowing a little overlap over the edges (you'll fold this in later). Keep laying the filo in the pan until you have a good sturdy 3- to 4-sheet layer all over—you may need to patch it together bit by bit if you have small sheets.

CONTINUED

## SERVES 4 TO 6

2 red onions

coconut or olive oil

1 pound/500 g butternut squash

leaves from ½ bunch of thyme

7 ounces/200 g of filo pastry

2 free-range or organic eggs

3½ ounces/100 g pecorino or Parmesan cheese (I use a vegetarian one)

freshly ground pepper

olive oil

7 ounces/200 g lacinato kale

1 unwaxed lemon

3½ ounces/100 g goat cheese

3½ ounces/100 g black olives (I use Kalamata), pitted

Once the squash has had 5 minutes, scoop it into a bowl. Crack in the eggs and grate in the pecorino or Parmesan. Season with pepper and mix well.

Drizzle the filo pastry with a little olive oil, then use a pastry brush to distribute the oil all over the pastry. Spoon the butternut mixture into the pan and put over medium heat.

Working quickly, shred the kale and toss it with the juice and zest of the lemon and a little oil. Scatter it on top of the butternut and push down a little into the mixture, then dot the goat cheese and olives on top. Fold the excess filo back over the filling to form a wavy edge. Place on the bottom rack of the oven and bake for 20 to 25 minutes, or until golden and crisp.

Take out of the oven, cut into six generous slices, and serve.

# Butternut and cannellini gratin

This is a favorite warming winter or autumn dinner. It's crispy-topped, with a sweet butternut, lemon, and herb filling. It's super easy to put together and is made from simple stuff that I usually have on hand.

Try experimenting with other squashes if you find them in the store, as they all cook in roughly the same amount of time. Mixing a few different colors and shapes can be really pretty and make it more interesting to eat.

If you are vegan, or if you just fancy changing this up, you can add a handful of chopped almonds in place of the cheese; it's not the same, but it's just as good.

Preheat your oven to 425°F/220°C (convection 400°F/200°C) and get all your ingredients and equipment together.

Coarsely slice the onions. Put a wide, shallow, ovenproof casserole pan over medium heat, add a good glug of olive oil, and fry the onions until soft and sweet.

Cut the squash into large dice, discarding the seeds (there is no need to peel), then add to the softened onions with the leaves from the rosemary sprigs and continue cooking until the squash has colored a little at the edges and is starting to soften; this will take about 10 minutes.

Take off the heat and add the drained cannellini beans, then season with salt and pepper and squeeze the juice of the lemon over.

Pour the stock over, then tear the bread over the top. Grate the Gruyère over the top, if you like. Bake for 35 to 45 minutes, until the cheese has melted and the stock is bubbling around the edges.

SERVES 6

3 red onions

olive oil

2 pounds/1 kg butternut or other orange-fleshed squash

a few sprigs of rosemary

2 (14-ounce/400-g) cans of cannellini beans, or 2¾ cups/ 500 g home-cooked beans (see pages 241–245)

sea salt and freshly ground pepper

1 lemon

1¼ cups/300 ml hot vegetable stock

3 thick slices of good sourdough or whole wheat bread

5 ounces/150 g Gruyère cheese

# Roasted coconut, lime, and tamarind curry

This recipe, like the sweet potato dal in *A Modern Way to Eat*, has become an instant classic in my house. I make this a lot, and each time I make it I still can't believe how tasty it is. The squash, fennel seeds, and tamarind come together to make a vibrant curry, and the toasted maple and lime coconut is the crowning glory (and a great little treat for snacking on in its own right).

If you are in a real rush, you could use precooked brown rice here. I usually keep some leftover rice in the freezer (see page 246 on cooking and storing grains), but if you search out one without any additives, the precooked pouches can be a speedy solution.

SERVES 4

1½ cups/300 g short-grain brown rice

1 red onion

coconut oil

2 cloves garlic

a thumb-sized piece of ginger

1 red chile

2 carrots

a large bunch of cilantro

14 ounces/400 g butternut, kabocha, or acorn squash

7 ounces/200 g spinach or other greens

1 tablespoon fennel seeds

1 tablespoon mustard seeds

1 (14-ounce/400-g) can of good chopped tomatoes

1 (14-ounce/400-g) can of coconut milk

2 tablespoons tamarind paste

17 ounces/500 g unsweetened coconut flakes or desiccated coconut

2 unwaxed limes

2 tablespoons maple syrup

Preheat your oven to 400°F/200°C (convection 375°F/180°C). Fill and boil a kettle of water and get all your ingredients together. Put a big saucepan over medium heat.

Get your rice on. Measure out the rice in a mug or measuring cup, making a note of the level it comes up to, then rinse it in cold water and put it into the pan. Fill the mug to the same level with water and add to the pan, then repeat so you have double the volume of water as rice. Add a good pinch of salt, bring to a boil, then turn down the heat and simmer for 20 minutes.

Meanwhile, finely chop the red onion. Put a teaspoon of coconut oil into another large saucepan, add the onion, and cook over high heat for 5 minutes, until soft.

Chop the garlic, ginger, and chile, and put to one side. Peel the carrots and chop into ¼-inch/5-mm rounds. Chop the cilantro stalks and put the leaves to one side. Once the onion is soft, add the garlic, ginger, chile, carrots, and cilantro stalks to the pan and cook for a couple of minutes.

CONTINUED

Cut the squash in half lengthwise (there is no need to peel) and then into quarters. Remove the seeds, then cut into thin ¼-inch/5-mm slices. Wash the spinach and remove any tough stalks.

Add the fennel and mustard seeds to the pan and allow to cook until the mustard seeds start popping, then add the squash, tomatoes, coconut milk, and tamarind paste. Put a lid on the pan and simmer over medium-high heat for 20 minutes, until you have a thick, flavorful curry. Top up with a little hot water from the kettle if it gets too thick.

Meanwhile, line a baking sheet with parchment paper. Put the coconut flakes on the sheet and grate over the zest of 1 lime. Pour over the maple syrup and put into the oven for 5 minutes, until turning golden at the edges.

When the rice is ready, drain it and keep it warm. Once the curry is cooked, stir in the spinach and the cilantro leaves and squeeze in the juice of both the limes. Spoon some rice into your bowls and ladle the curry over the top. Scatter the roasted coconut on top and finish with the cilantro leaves.

# A modern moussaka

I first ate this in L.A. and I have dreamed of it ever since. It's rich, creamy, and tasty at the same time as feeling bright and clean.

Be sure to cook your eggplant through on the grill pan, as there are few things worse than raw eggplant. It will be translucent and soft all the way through when it's ready.

I have kept this dish naturally vegan and dairy free, as I find it lighter and more delicious. You could easily swap the coconut oil for butter and almond milk for cow's milk, to make a more classic béchamel. Serve this with some bright, lemon-dressed leaves.

........................................................................................................................................

Preheat the oven to 425°F/220°C (convection 400°F/200°C) and heat a grill pan on high heat. Fill and boil a kettle of water and get all your ingridients and equipment together.

Halve the tomatoes and finely slice the onions. On a large rimmed baking sheet, toss them with a drizzle of olive oil, scatter over the chile, grate over the zest of the lemon, and add a little salt and pepper. Put them into the oven to roast for 20 minutes.

Cook the potatoes in boiling water from the kettle for 12 to 15 minutes, until tender and cooked through.

Meanwhile, slice the eggplants into ¼-inch/5-mm rounds. Cook them in the hot grill pan until cooked through and charred on both sides—you will need to do this in batches. Put each cooked batch on a plate, drizzle with a little olive oil, and season with salt and pepper.

⁘ CONTINUED

SERVES 4 TO 6

17 ounces/500 g cherry tomatoes

2 red onions

olive oil

a pinch of dried chile flakes

1 lemon

sea salt and freshly ground pepper

1⅓ pounds/600 g small new potatoes

2 eggplants

3 tablespoons coconut oil

3 tablespoons spelt flour

1¼ cups/300 ml unsweetened almond milk

To make the béchamel, melt the coconut oil in a saucepan, add the flour, and cook for a couple of minutes to cook out the rawness, then add the almond milk bit by bit, whisking as you go to make sure there are no lumps. It should be a pretty thick béchamel, similar to Greek yogurt.

Drain the potatoes. Put a large, shallow, heavy-bottomed ovenproof pan on medium-high heat and add 3 tablespoons of olive oil, then add the potatoes. Use a potato masher to squash them a tiny bit so they have a flat side underneath; leave them to brown a little. Toss every now and then so they are crisp but not sticking to the pan. Season well.

Once the bottoms of the potatoes are brown, take the tomatoes out of the oven and spoon over the potatoes. Top with the grilled eggplant and spoon the béchamel over. Heat the broiler to high and put the pan under the broiler for 5 to 10 minutes.

Once the casserole is browned and bubbling, serve in the middle of the table.

# Crispy chickpea and harissa burgers

These burgers are easy to fall for: super simple to put together, highly spiced, and with a backnote of sweetness from the dates. I make a double batch and freeze half for quick dinners throughout the week.

Don't be tempted to skip the relish; it really makes these burgers sing. If you can't get pomegranate molasses or it's a step too far for you, a tablespoon of honey mixed with a tablespoon of punchy balsamic vinegar will stand in for it.

........................................................................................

Fill and boil a kettle of water and get all your ingredients together.

If you need to cook your quinoa, start by toasting it in a pan until you can hear it pop, as this gives it more flavor. Then put it into a mug or measuring cup, making a note of the level it comes up to, and pour it into a large pan. Fill the mug to the same level with boiling water and add to the pan, then repeat so you have double the volume of water as quinoa. Cook until all the water has been absorbed and the little curly grains have been released from each quinoa seed.

Put the frozen peas into a heatproof bowl, cover them with boiling water, and leave them to sit for 10 minutes.

Put the drained chickpeas into a frying pan with the cumin, coriander, and smoked paprika and toast until all the moisture has gone and they are starting to pop.

Drain the peas very well and put them back into the dry bowl. Tip in half the chickpeas and half the cooked quinoa, then add the dates, parsley, harissa, and mustard and use a handheld blender to blend until everything is combined. Stir in the rest of the chickpeas and quinoa and mix well.

Divide the mixture into six and shape each one into a burger. Pop them into the fridge to firm up.

SERVES 6

**FOR THE BURGERS**
7 ounces/200 g cooked quinoa (3½ ounces/100 g uncooked)
7 ounces/200 g frozen peas
1 (14-ounce/400-g) can of chickpeas or 1½ cups/250 g home-cooked chickpeas (see pages 241–245)
1 teaspoon ground cumin
1 teaspoon ground coriander
½ teaspoon smoked paprika
4 medjool dates
a large bunch of parsley
1 tablespoon harissa
1 tablespoon Dijon mustard
olive or coconut oil
1¾ ounces/50 g sesame seeds

**FOR THE RELISH**
1 red onion
7 ounces/200 g cherry tomatoes
a good drizzle of pomegranate molasses
a bunch of cilantro

**TO SERVE**
6 good burger buns
hummus
salad leaves

To make the relish, finely slice the onion and fry in oil over high heat for 8 to 10 minutes, until soft and sweet. Add the chopped tomatoes and cook for another 5 minutes, until they have broken down, then add the pomegranate molasses. Take off the heat and transfer to a bowl, then coarsely chop the cilantro and mix in.

While the relish is cooking, you can get on with cooking your burgers. Heat a frying pan over medium heat (you can cook them in batches or have two pans on the go if you prefer). Add a little olive or coconut oil and fry the burgers on each side for 5 minutes, until crisp and warmed through. Once they are done, sprinkle both sides with sesame seeds and cook for another minute on each side to toast. You can also bake the burgers on an oiled baking sheet at 425°F/220°C (convection 400°F/200°C) for 20 to 25 minutes.

Warm the buns in a dry pan and layer the burgers with the hummus, some tomato relish, and the salad leaves.

# Honey and white miso eggplant

Eggplant and mushrooms fall into the same territory for me: unless they are cooked perfectly I am not interested. So I am very selective with the eggplant recipes that make it to my kitchen, let alone to this book. This one is a knockout, everything an eggplant should be—soft and buttery on the inside, and burnished and just crisp on the outside. The miso paste that is generously spread on top is a fanfare of flavor. I serve this with brown sushi rice, which I buy in a Japanese supermarket or online. It can be hard to come by—white sushi rice will work in a pinch.

Get all your ingredients together and preheat the broiler to medium.

First, cook the sushi rice. This is how I like to do it: wash the sushi rice three or four times in cold water, until the water runs clear, then add 1⅔ cups/400 ml of cold water and bring to a boil. Put a lid on and boil for 10 to 15 minutes for white rice and 15 to 20 minutes for brown, then turn the heat off and leave the lid on. Don't peek, as this will release the steam, which you need to finish the cooking.

Cut the eggplants in half lengthwise, then cut the flesh in a crisscross pattern without cutting into the skin. Brush both sides of each eggplant with the oil. Place on a rimmed baking sheet cut side down and broil for 5 minutes, then turn them over and broil for a further 5 minutes, until soft all the way through. Turn the oven to 425°F/220°C (convection 400°F/200°C) and turn off the broiler. Mix the white and dark miso in a bowl with the honey, mirin, chile powder, and a tablespoon of hot water. Rub the cut side of the eggplants with the miso mixture and put back into the oven to cook for 15 minutes.

Heat a pan with a little coconut oil and sauté the kale and bok choy until just cooked, then toss with the soy and the yuzu or lime juice. Take the eggplants out of the oven and sprinkle with the sesame seeds. Take the lid off the rice and stir in the brown rice vinegar. Serve the rice topped with the greens, eggplants, and the sticky sauce from the baking sheet spooned over. Top with more sesame seeds if you like.

SERVES 4 TO 6

1½ cups/300 g brown sushi rice

4 long, slim eggplants

1 tablespoon melted coconut oil, plus a little extra

2 tablespoons white miso paste

2 tablespoons dark miso paste

2 tablespoons runny honey

2 tablespoons mirin

a healthy pinch of chile powder

1 bunch of kale
(about 7 ounces/200 g)

4 bunches bok choy

a splash of soy sauce or tamari

1 tablespoon yuzu lime juice or the juice of 1 lime

4 tablespoons toasted black and white sesame seeds

2 tablespoons brown rice or rice wine vinegar

investment
cooking

This kind of cooking is the backbone of my kitchen—smart cooking that means I have some nourishing, delicious food to help me through the week. You don't have to do this every week, but when you have an hour or so to spare, this kind of cooking can soothe your soul and help you put quick suppers together during the week—not to mention a few treats. Nut butters and tahini, sweet treats, quick granolas, the best banana bread you'll ever taste, miraculous chickpea tofu from scratch, vats of grains and beans, stocks, soups, my favorite rye bread, and homemade coconut yogurt.

heavenly nut butters · blood orange and double chocolate rye muffins · malted chocolate buckwheat granola · start as you mean to go on cereal · ultimate pecan banana breakfast bread · make-your-own chickpea tofu · perfect home-cooked beans · amazing grains · quick homemade paneer · a sunday vat of soup · making good vegetable stock · honey rye bread · how to make tahini · three vibrant dips · amazing crackers · coconut yogurt · homemade milks from nuts, oats, and seeds · rainbow paletas · carrot cake granola bars · summer rhubarb and strawberry crisp bars · amazing lemon cannellini cake · sweet potato and malted chocolate cake

# Heavenly nut butters

There is so much joy in making something at home that you usually buy, an unparalleled feeling of smugness. My favorite thing about making pantry staples at home, though, is the freedom to make things that are truly original, to mix flavors you can't find anywhere else, and tweak and blend things just to my taste.

That is exactly what has happened here. I am in love with nut butter. I eat it on toast or rice cakes for a quick snack, dip fruit in it, use it in dressings, and spoon it onto my morning porridge. I often make simple almond butter with a pinch of salt, which is a staple ingredient. These butters are a lot more special, though; they use stellar combinations of flavors at the same time as being raw and nutrient-packed, so you can be sure that you are boosting the flavor and goodness of your meals every time you open a jar.

I've included three different-flavored nut butters here. Coconut and Cardamom Almond Butter is a particular favorite of mine. I find it hard to leave the jar alone. If lucuma is hard to find, or one step too far, you can leave it out. The Salted Date Caramel Pecan Butter is a salted caramel that is acceptable to eat for breakfast, and the Hazelnut and Cacao Butter is just better Nutella. To make a simple, unflavored nut butter, you can use raw, roasted, or activated (see below) nuts and blend them to a butter as these methods explain. A little salt and sometimes a splash of water are good additions.

You can make these with raw nuts and they will be delicious, but for maximum nutrition I recommend activating the nuts. To do this, soak the nuts overnight in cold water, drain and rinse, then dry out in the oven at its lowest temperature for 4 hours, until completely dry. A good trick here is to leave the oven door slightly ajar so all the moisture can escape. Activating your nuts

CONTINUED

sounds a bit silly, but it is basically a way of boosting their nutritional value. First you soak them in water, which tricks the nuts into thinking they are about to grow into a plant, so all their nutrients are released. Then you gently heat them to dry them out, so that they can be kept for longer—the soaked nuts only last a couple of days.

For a smooth nut butter, you need a good food processor or high-speed blender. If you don't have one of these, a crunchy texture can be achieved using a hand blender.

Get all your ingredients together for whichever nut butter you are making. If using coconut oil, melt it and let it cool. A hot spoon will help you measure the coconut oil more easily. If you like your nut butter crunchy, spoon out 2 heaped tablespoons before it's completely smooth (you'll stir this through at the end).

Place the nuts in your food processor or blender and pulse until you have a fine powder. You will need to stop the food processor and use a spatula to scrape down the sides from time to time. This should take 2 to 4 minutes, depending on how powerful your machine is.

Once the nuts begin to form a paste, add the rest of the ingredients except the water and blend until you have a smooth butter—you may need to scrape down the sides again a few times.

Add the water and blend again. Top up with a little extra water if necessary, until your nut butter is the consistency you like. Scoop out of the processor; if you have reserved some crunchy nuts, put the nut butter into a bowl, add the crunchy nuts, and beat together. Then spoon the butter into sterilized jars (see page 257). Keeps in a cool place for up to 6 weeks.

## COCONUT AND CARDAMOM ALMOND BUTTER

10 ounces/300 g raw skin-on almonds (activated if you like—see headnote)

3½ ounces/100 g creamed coconut

¼ cup/50 g coconut sugar

2 tablespoons lucuma powder (optional)

1 teaspoon vanilla extract

seeds from 4 cardamom pods, bashed

seeds from 2 vanilla pods

½ to ⅔ cup/100 to 150 ml water

## HAZELNUT AND CACAO BUTTER

10 ounces/300 g raw skinned hazelnuts (activated if you like—see headnote)

4 tablespoons maple syrup

4 tablespoons coconut oil or cacao butter

4 tablespoons cocoa powder or cacao nibs

½ to ⅔ cup/100 to 150 ml water

## SALTED DATE CARAMEL PECAN BUTTER

10 ounces/300 g raw pecans (activated if you like—see headnote)

10 pitted medjool dates

a good pinch of salt

½ to ⅔ cup/100 to 150 ml water

# Blood orange and double chocolate rye muffins

This is like a Terry's Chocolate Orange ball in a healthier muffin version that you can happily eat for breakfast. Either you are with me on this one, or you'll have already turned the page.

These little guys have no refined sugar, no dairy, and just a bit of spelt and rye flour. You could easily use a good gluten-free flour if you preferred, which works really well, as the milk and oil keep the muffins from drying out.

You can keep these pretty lean, but when I want to make them more of a treat, adding 3½ ounces/ 100 g of chopped dark chocolate sprinkled over at the end adds some gooey melting goodness. I use blood oranges when they are in the grocery store, but a normal orange will work just fine too.

..............................................................................

Preheat the oven to 425°F/220°C (convection 400°F/ 200°C). Line the cups of a muffin pan with paper liners. Get all your ingredients together. If you are using coconut oil, melt it and let it cool.

Sift together all the dry ingredients in a large mixing bowl.

Crack the eggs in a separate bowl and whisk together, then add the milk, maple syrup, and oil while constantly stirring. Grate in the zest of one of the oranges.

Use a knife to cut the peel from both oranges and remove any pithy bits, then chop the oranges

**MAKES 12 MUFFINS**

⅔ cup/150 ml olive oil or coconut oil

1¼ cups/150 g good white spelt flour

⅓ cup/50 g whole-grain rye flour

5 tablespoons cocoa powder
(I use the raw stuff)

1 teaspoon baking powder

3 free-range organic eggs

1 cup/250 ml milk of your choice
(I use drinking coconut milk)

⅔ cup/150 ml pure maple syrup

2 unwaxed blood oranges or normal oranges

3½ ounces/100 g dark chocolate (70 percent)

⁙ CONTINUED

into small pieces, taking care to cut out any bits of white pith from the center.

Add the dry mixture to the wet mixture. Coarsely chop the dark chocolate and add half of it to the batter, along with half the orange pieces. Use a spatula to carefully fold everything together until combined.

Divide the batter among the muffin cups and top with the rest of the dark chocolate and orange pieces. Bake for 16 to 18 minutes. Best warm from the oven.

# Malted chocolate buckwheat granola

My formative years in America led to an obsession with malted chocolate milkshakes. In fact malted chocolate anything. I don't go for the milkshakes much anymore, but I still crave that chocolate and malt combo. This is my solution, a health-packed granola that has the bonus of creating a chocolate malt milkshake in the bottom of my bowl.

You can use more maple syrup in place of the barley malt here, but you'll miss out on the malty taste. Barley malt syrup can be found in all health food shops and is a naturally processed sweetener made up of about 50 percent maltose, a sugar that is only about one-third as sweet as white sugar. It still retains many nutrients from the barley grain from which it was made, and this type of complex sugar takes longer to digest, so it won't give you the sugar highs and lows of a Mars bar.

This granola is great for a quick sweet snack—I eat it on its own with almond milk and a scattering of raspberries—but it's just as good with yogurt or on top of a bowl of porridge to liven things up a little.

.....................................................

Preheat the oven to 350°F/180°C (convection 325°F/160°C) and get all your ingredients together.

In a generously sized bowl, mix the oats, buckwheat, dried fruit, cocoa powder, and chia seeds. Coarsely chop the pecans and add these too.

Put the maple syrup, barley malt syrup, and coconut oil into a pan and warm through.

Pour the syrup mixture over the oat mixture and mix until it's all coated. Then put on a large rimmed baking

⋮ CONTINUED

MAKES A GOOD JARFUL
(ABOUT 1¾ POUNDS/800 G)

3 cups/300 g rolled oats

1¼ cups/200 g buckwheat seeds

3½ ounces/100 g dried fruit (I use coconut flakes, chopped dates, raisins, or chopped apricots)

4 tablespoons cocoa powder

3 tablespoons/30 g chia seeds

4 ounces/125 g pecans

¼ cup/60 ml maple syrup

4 tablespoons barley malt syrup

¼ cup/60 ml melted coconut oil

sheet or two smaller ones and squish it all together with your hands to form little bundles of granola.

Put into the oven for 5 to 10 minutes, then take the granola out and use a spoon or spatula to roughly break it up a bit. Put back into the oven for a further 5 to 10 minutes.

It's done when it starts to form lovely crunchy bundles. The dark color from the cocoa will mean it's easy to overcook, as you won't be able to see, so if anything, take it out a little earlier if you think it's ready.

# Start as you mean to go on cereal

I make this cereal blend and keep it in a big jar in my kitchen, so that when mornings are short, rushed, bleary, or fraught, I know that I can scoop some of this into a pan and 20 minutes later have something fortifying and nourishing that will set me up for the rest of my waking hours. I often use rye flakes or even buckwheat seeds in place of the oats.

If I can, I try to soak my cereal overnight in a little water with a squeeze of lemon juice. If you don't remember, or you think that's a bridge too far, don't worry about it.

I have given three ideas for toppings below: two sweet, one savory, all delicious.

**FOR THE MIX**
Mix all the ingredients in a large jar, or mix in a bowl and divide between two smaller jars, and store for up to 3 months.

**TO COOK**
Mix about ¼ cup/50 g of the mixture per person with 1 cup/250 ml of water or a mixture of water and unsweetened almond milk. Bring to a boil, then simmer for 15 to 20 minutes until cooked and creamy.

**TOPPING IDEAS**
· Sliced persimmon, pomegranate, dates, and chopped pistachios
· Grated apple, nutmeg, cinnamon, and chopped almonds
· Poached egg, chile, and toasted sesame seeds

MAKES ABOUT 20 PORTIONS

1 cup/90 g oats (gluten-free if needed)
1 cup/200 g millet flakes
1 cup/170 g quinoa flakes
1 cup/190 g amaranth
¼ cup/40 g chia seeds
¼ cup/30 g poppy seeds

# Ultimate pecan banana breakfast bread

This is my ultimate banana bread. Soft, moist, and light all at once, with a topping of seeds that would make any Swedish baker proud and studded with chunks of darkest chocolate. All without any gluten, dairy, eggs, or refined sugar. So toast this for breakfast with wild abandon and congratulate yourself for making something that is insanely indulgent tasting and incredibly delicious without dragging you down.

This bread is also just as good and a bit more virtuous without the chocolate. I add chocolate if I'm making it for teatime but otherwise I leave it out and it becomes our breakfast for the week. Much better than a piece of toast or a bowl of porridge. If you can't find coconut sugar, you could use light brown sugar here.

..................................................................................................

Preheat the oven to 350°F/170°C (convection 300°F/ 150°C) and get all your ingredients together. Grease a 2-pound/900-g nonstick loaf pan with coconut oil.

While the oven comes up to temperature, roast the pecans in it for 10 minutes, then coarsely chop and set aside. Meanwhile, pulse the oats in a food processor until you have a scruffy flour. Put the oat flour into a bowl.

Put the bananas into the food processor with the ⅔ cup/100 g of coconut sugar, maple syrup, almond milk, and melted coconut oil and blitz until well combined. Add the oat flour, baking powder, and salt. Blend until combined, then stir in the pecans. Add the caraway seeds, if using.

Pour half the batter into the loaf pan. Break the chocolate up into thin strips and lay it along the middle of the batter, leaving space at the end. Pour in the rest of the batter and top with the extra spoonful of coconut sugar. Bake for 70 minutes, or until a skewer comes out clean. Leave to cool on a wire rack for at least 30 minutes.

MAKES 1 GOOD 2-POUND/900-G LOAF

¼ cup/75 ml melted coconut oil, plus extra for greasing

7 ounces/200 g pecans (walnuts work too)

2 cups/200 g rolled oats

4 large ripe bananas

⅔ cup/100 g coconut sugar, plus 1 tablespoon (optional)

scant ½ cup/100 ml maple syrup

scant ½ cup/100 ml unsweetened almond milk

2 teaspoons baking powder

a good pinch of salt

a good pinch of caraway seeds (optional)

2½ ounces/75 g dark chocolate (70 percent)

# Make-your-own chickpea tofu

It can be hard to get your hands on really good tofu at the supermarkets. I think part of the reason many people turn their noses up at it is because they haven't had the good stuff.

As we all know, much soy is grown in industrialized, often GMO, farms, so in my quest to throw the nutritional net as wide as possible, I looked to chickpeas. Chickpea tofu is a staple of Burmese kitchens. It's more flavorful than regular tofu, but is still neutral enough that it could be paired with Asian, Indian, or even Italian flavors.

This recipe does take a bit of planning, as the chickpea flour needs to soak for 1 to 2 days. It also makes a big, family-size amount. If there are only a couple of you in the house, I'd suggest halving the quantities.

......................................................................

In a very large saucepan (one that will take about 4 quarts/4 liters), combine the chickpea flour and water. Place a clean kitchen towel over the top and leave it to sit somewhere not too warm, where it will not be disturbed. Let it sit for about 24 hours; you may need to soak it a little less in a warmer climate.

After the soaking time, uncover the saucepan; the chickpea flour will have started to ferment a little, so there may be a slight fermentation smell. Without stirring or moving the saucepan, carefully remove 4 cups/1 liter of water from the top of the mixture with a ladle or measuring cup and discard.

In a medium pan, melt the oil over medium heat. Carefully pour in the remaining liquid without disturbing the bottom too much and stopping when you get to the thick chickpea paste at the bottom.

⠿ CONTINUED

MAKES ABOUT 3 POUNDS/1.5 KG

FOR THE BASIC TOFU
3½ cups/350 g chickpea flour
3½ quarts/3½ liters cold water
½ tablespoon coconut oil
2½ teaspoons fine sea salt

OPTIONAL FLAVORINGS
**Smoked**
replace the sea salt with smoked salt

**Spiced**
1 tablespoon ground turmeric
1 teaspoon ground coriander

**Herbed**
a small bunch of thyme,
leaves picked and very finely chopped

a small bunch of oregano,
leaves picked and very finely chopped

This paste stays in the saucepan and it'll be what you will use to thicken the mixture shortly.

Add the salt, and a flavoring, if you are using one, and whisk well to combine. Cook over medium heat, stirring frequently, for 15 to 20 minutes, until the mixture begins to simmer and thicken.

Add the chickpea paste from the saucepan and keep stirring vigorously with a wooden spoon. After about 6 or 7 minutes, the mixture will thicken to the consistency of a cake batter. Cook for a further 10 minutes to cook out the flour; you'll need to keep stirring to keep the bottom from burning.

Line an 9 by 13-inch/20 by 30-cm baking dish with a clean cotton kitchen towel or cheesecloth. Pour the thickened chickpea mixture into the baking dish and smooth the surface. Fold the edges of the cloth over the top and let it sit at room temperature for about 6 hours.

To remove the tofu from the dish, place a cutting board on top and flip it over, then pull the cloth away. Cut into meal-sized chunks of about 7 ounces/200 g each and keep in the fridge for up to 5 days. Keep the tofu on a dish, as it can let out a little water while it's stored in the fridge. Unfortunately, this tofu doesn't freeze too well.

To fry your chickpea tofu, use a nonstick pan and a little oil to keep it from sticking—it is a little bit more prone to sticking than normal tofu.

# Perfect home-cooked beans

Cooking dried beans may not sound like the most enchanting or exciting thing to do in a recipe, or even anything new. But cooking beans this way has seriously changed how I do things in my kitchen and how delicious my meals are, how much time it takes to put them together, and how much they cost.

Beans are an amazing ingredient to include in your diet. They are high in complex carbohydrates and fiber, high in protein, and low in fat, while being loaded with vitamins.

I have moved from using canned beans to cooking my own, from scratch, in big batches and freezing them cleverly in portions, ready to make into hummus, soups, or stews. They are so much more delicious and buttery cooked at home, and the process is one I love—running your hands through a bowl of dried beans is so satisfying, as is opening a freezer drawer packed with ready-to-go little bags of beans.

It is worth mentioning that the length of time it takes to cook a dried bean will depend on how long ago it was dried. The older it is, the longer it will take to cook. I would encourage you to buy beans from places where they are less likely to have been sitting around for a long time: anywhere that has loose beans to buy by weight is a good option.

If you want to find out more about beans and other pulses, get yourself a copy of the brilliant book *Pulse* by Jenny Chandler, which is a pulse bible and has inspired some of the following techniques.

A note on beans and protein: the protein we get from beans is not a complete protein like the ones found in eggs, quinoa, buckwheat, and chia seeds. Beans have

CONTINUED

only seven of the eight amino acids which make up a complete protein. But the missing piece of the jigsaw can be filled by grains or sesame seeds, which contain the eighth amino acid. So eating your beans with a little bread (see page 254) or in hummus (with tahini; see page 257) will form a complete protein, which will provide more energy and nourishment for your body.

### SOAKING

Most beans will benefit from a little overnight soak in double their volume of fresh cold (ideally filtered) water. Soaking beans makes them much easier to digest and reduces their famous side effects as well as their cooking time; it also allows them to cook more evenly.

If you don't have time to soak your beans, don't fret, as there are a couple of other options. Either give them a quick soak, for as much time as you have but ideally for 2 hours, or cook them without soaking—though in my experience the time you save by not soaking them will only be replaced by the extra time they take to cook.

### COOKING

To cook, drain the soaked beans, put them into your largest pan, and cover with cold water to come about 1¼ inches/3 cm above the level of the beans. Bring to a boil, then boil steadily for 5 minutes (10 for kidney beans)—this is important, as it deactivates the toxins in the beans—then turn down the heat to a very gentle simmer and cook until tender and creamy. Cooking over low heat like this will ensure the skins stay intact and that the beans cook evenly. It is better to shake your pan rather than stir with a wooden spoon, as stirring will break the skins of the beans.

⋮ CONTINUED

A cooked bean should remain intact but should collapse into a buttery, creamy mush when squeezed. Chickpeas will remain a little harder but should still be soft throughout.

I season my beans once they are cooked, as seasoning them while cooking is said to toughen the beans and give them a powdery texture. They do need a good bit of seasoning once they come off the heat.

**FREEZING**

You can freeze your cooled beans in their cooking liquid, in portions as they would come in a can, but I prefer to freeze them without their liquid. I season them well, then drain the liquid and allow the beans to cool before freezing them in meal-sized bags. If I have time, I freeze them on a tray first, to stop them from sticking together, and bag them up once frozen.

## SOAKING AND COOKING TIMES FOR DRIED BEANS AND OTHER PULSES

### QUICK

**SOAK 30 MINUTES +
COOKING 30 TO 40 MINUTES**

Lentils and split peas
Mung beans

### SHORT

**SOAK 2 TO 3 HOURS +
COOKING 30 TO 40 MINUTES**

Adzuki beans
Black-eyed peas

### MEDIUM

**SOAK 4 HOURS +
COOKING 1 TO 1½ HOURS**

Borlotti beans
Cannellini beans
Kidney beans
Lima beans
Navy beans
Pinto beans

### LONG

**SOAK 8 HOURS OR OVERNIGHT +
COOKING 1½ TO 3 HOURS**

Chickpeas
Fava beans
Soybeans

# Amazing grains

Grains and so-called pseudo-grains like quinoa and amaranth (which look and cook like grains but are actually seeds) are a big part of how I like to eat, but quite a few of them take a while to cook, so I like to cook them in big batches and have them in my fridge or freezer for whenever I need something quickly.

Eating a range of grains means that you are introducing a wide spectrum of vitamins and minerals into your diet.

These days you can also buy packages of precooked grains in supermarkets and delis, though they vary wildly in quality and in what has been added to them. If you find a reliable brand, these can be a good option if you are in a fix.

### SOAKING

These grains and pseudo-grains, like beans and nuts, benefit from soaking. It will speed up their cooking time, maximize their nutritional value, and make them easier to digest. An overnight soak in double the amount of cold (ideally filtered) water is ideal, but a couple of hours is good too— and if you don't have time, it's not the end of the world.

### COOKING

Drain your soaked grain and put into a large pot with the specified amount of liquid. I cook all my grains in vegetable stock, which adds flavor and depth. I often also squeeze the juice of a lemon into the pan, then put the squeezed halves into the pan while the grain cooks to add extra flavor. Cook until tender.

### STORING AND FREEZING

Drain your grains and cool well—if you want to speed this up, you can cool them on a couple of baking sheets. They can then be stored for 3 to 4 days in the fridge, or frozen in portions for super-quick dinners.

### QUINOA—RED, BLACK, AND WHITE

You'll need 2 cups of water to 1 cup of quinoa. I like to dry-toast my quinoa in a pan before cooking until it starts to make a popping sound— this adds a deeper, toasty flavor. Cook for about 12 minutes, until all the water has been absorbed and the little curly grain has popped out of each seed. I like to keep the pan on the heat until I can just hear the popping sound again, to make sure all the water is gone.

### BROWN RICE

Rinse your rice under running cold water. For 1 cup of uncooked rice you'll need 1¼ cups of water for long-grain and 1½ for brown rice. Bring to a boil, then reduce to a steady simmer and cook for 30 minutes, until the rice is tender. Drain and leave in the pan to steam for a further 10 minutes.

### AMARANTH

You'll need 2½ cups of water for every cup of amaranth. Bring to a boil, then simmer for 20 minutes, until the grains are fluffy and the liquid has been absorbed.

### BUCKWHEAT

Buckwheat comes in two forms: kasha, which is toasted, and buckwheat groats, which are untoasted. I usually use the raw groats. First rinse your groats under running cold water until it runs clear. Then you'll need 2 cups of liquid for each cup of groats. Bring to a boil, then simmer for 20 to 30 minutes, until tender, 15 to 20 if you use toasted buckwheat or kasha. If you like, you can toast the groats yourself, in a dry pan, for 1 to 2 minutes, until they smell nutty.

### MILLET

You'll need 2½ cups of water for every cup of millet. Bring to a boil, then simmer for 25 minutes, until the grains are fluffy and the liquid has been absorbed. Fluff up with a fork. You can toast millet in a pan before cooking to add a nutty flavor in the same way as quinoa.

### FARRO

You'll need 2 cups of water to every cup of farro. Bring to a boil, then simmer for 30 minutes, until tender. Farro contains gluten.

### PEARLED BARLEY

You'll need 3 cups of water to each cup of barley. Bring to a boil, then turn the heat down and simmer for 45 to 50 minutes, until tender. Pearled barley contains gluten.

### FREEKEH

Freekeh is immature wheat that is harvested while still young and soft, then roasted or sun-dried. The health bonus of harvesting immature wheat is that it retains more of its nutrients and proteins than its fully grown counterparts. It even claims to have fewer carbohydrates than regular wheat.

Wash the grain first by swirling in water and rubbing the grains together vigorously. Drain and repeat until the water is clear. You'll need 2 cups of water for every cup of freekeh. Bring to a boil, cover, and simmer until the water is completely absorbed (about 15 minutes for cracked grain and 45 minutes for whole grain). Remove from the heat and use a fork to fluff up.

# Quick homemade paneer

This is one of the most pleasing things to make at home—the white curds wrapped in cheesecloth are so satisfying in their clean white simplicity.

I like making my own paneer, as that way I can use really good organic milk. Homemade paneer is a good bit cheaper than the store-bought stuff and, of course, the flavor and texture are much more delicate. If you are making paneer for a crowd, you can double this recipe, but this makes a perfect amount for a meal for four.

MAKES ABOUT 14 OUNCES/400 G

2 quarts/2 liters full-fat organic milk
juice of 2 lemons

Pour the milk into a high-sided saucepan and place over medium heat. Bring to a boil, stirring every now and again so the milk doesn't form a skin.

Meanwhile, place a piece of cheesecloth or a clean kitchen towel over a large bowl and set aside.

When the milk starts to boil and to rise in the pan, add the lemon juice and stir until all the milk curds have formed. Remove from the heat and use a slotted spoon to scoop all the curds out of the milk into the muslin or cloth. Bring the edges of the cheesecloth together in your hands, then twist and carefully squeeze out any excess moisture from the curds.

Lay the bundle on a plate and squash down with something heavy; I use a large mortar and pestle. Leave for 40 minutes to set and you are ready to cook.

If you are not using the paneer straight away, place it in a bowl and cover with water. It will keep for up to 5 days in the fridge.

# A Sunday vat of soup

Life is busy, and even as someone who spends her life cooking, I often don't take as much time as I would like to make sure I am really well nourished. Some weeks I am saintly; I get in a rhythm and make breakfasts, lunches, and dinners to be proud of. Other weeks I don't do so well; it's in those weeks that I always try to make a pot of soup, and it's not always on a Sunday. I make it in my biggest pot so that we can have eight servings of easy goodness throughout the week.

This soup has a simple, nourishing character to it. It's made from sweet potatoes and squash, which are good sources of the kind of carbohydrates our bodies love, and are packed with beta-carotene and vitamins. I pair them with fennel seeds, which help digestion, and some chile to boost the metabolism and warm things up.

With one soup, there are a million things you can do. I find it difficult to eat the same thing night after night, so I use the soup as the base for a few different meals, adding different toppings and extras each night to make it seem new. Below are a few ideas of how to make one pot of soup into lots of different dinners.

The first day I tend to eat it puréed and smooth, straight up, with a quick herb oil and some bread. The second night I eat the soup with texture—I add some canned cannellini beans and top with some chopped chile. The next night I serve it with brown rice, yogurt, cilantro, and green chile. The possibilities are endless, and if you do get bored, you can freeze it in portions for a quick dinner when time is tight.

........................................................................

Fill and boil a kettle of water and get all your ingredients together. Get your biggest pot out—if you don't have a big enough pot, two smaller ones will do.

CONTINUED

SERVES 8

1 leek

1 red onion

2 carrots

2 celery stalks

olive oil or coconut oil

2 medium sweet potatoes

1 medium butternut squash

1 tablespoon fennel seeds

1 tablespoon Turkish chile or a good pinch of red chile flakes

1 tablespoon vegetable stock powder or 1 stock cube

Wash and finely slice the leek, and finely slice the onion, carrots, and celery.

Heat a large pan over medium heat and add a little olive or coconut oil. Once the pan is hot, add the chopped vegetables and cook for 10 to 15 minutes, until soft and sweet.

Meanwhile, peel the sweet potatoes and chop into large chunks. Seed the squash and coarsely chop into similar-size chunks (I leave the skin on, but if you like, you could peel this too).

Once the leek mixture is soft and smelling good, add the sweet potatoes, squash, and spices along with 2 quarts/ 2 liters of hot water from the kettle and the stock powder or cube. Bring to a boil, then turn down to a simmer and cook for 30 to 40 minutes, until the vegetables are soft and falling apart, topping up with a little hot water from the kettle if it starts to look a little thick.

I cool the lot and store it in the fridge or freezer until I'm hungry. I store it all without puréeing, as I like to eat it both silky smooth and with a more stewlike texture, so I warm and purée it in portions as I need.

### HERE ARE SOME OF THE WAYS I LIKE TO EAT MY VAT OF SOUP

- Blended until smooth, topped with a quick basil oil, and served with good bread.
- Stew-style, with some cannellini beans added while the soup is warming, and topped with crispy fried thyme bread crumbs and red chile.
- Half blended, warmed, and served over brown rice with chopped chile, cilantro, lime zest, and a spoonful of yogurt.
- Stew-style, with some smoked paprika stirred in while the soup is warming and topped with broken corn tortillas, red chile, and some little bits of avocado.

# Making good vegetable stock

This recipe is one from *A Modern Way to Eat*. It's a favorite in my house and still my preferred way to make stock. I use organic bouillon when I'm in a fix but I always try to have a jar of this in the fridge to ladle into soups and broths.

You'll need two 1-quart/1-liter preserving jars that will fit into your fridge. Don't feel tied to the amounts of vegetables below—the great thing about stock is that you can use up all the trimmings and odds and ends you have in the fridge. Just work to the same ratio, half-filling your liter jars with vegetables.

..................................................................................

Fill up a kettle of water and boil it. Divide the chopped vegetables and other ingredients between two 1-quart/1-liter jars. Fill the jars with the just-boiled water, leaving a 1-inch/2-cm gap at the top—each jar should hold about 3 cups/750 ml. Pop the lids on and leave in a safe place to cool down.

Strain straight away for a light stock, or put into the fridge for 12 hours and then strain for a more full-bodied stock.

Once the stock is strained, pour it back into the jars and store in the fridge, where it will keep for up to a week, or in a freezer.

MAKES 2 QUARTS/2 LITERS

2 carrots, coarsely chopped
1 red onion, cut into wedges
1 leek, cut into rounds
2 celery stalks, coarsely chopped
2 bay leaves, scrunched
a small bunch of thyme
1 teaspoon sea salt
a few black peppercorns

# Honey rye bread

I can't live without a good loaf of bread in the house. Real bread and gluten get shunned as unhealthy and out of bounds for a lot of people who are trying to eat consciously and healthily. I believe that a good, carefully made loaf of bread is a joy we should never try to live without (unless of course we have a serious intolerance). Many people's bad reaction to bread could be because of the quality of the bread they are eating. Like anything else, a good loaf needs good ingredients, some time, and a lot of love.

I believe in varying the grains I eat, and I find whole-grain flours more delicious and much more nourishing. So here is my current favorite loaf: half spelt and half rye, with a little honey, lots of seeds, and some caraway on top if that's your thing. Slicing a warm loaf of homemade bread satisfies and nourishes me in a way a thousand green juices couldn't.

........................................................................................

Get all your ingredients together. Put the flours into a warm, generously sized mixing bowl with the salt and mix well.

Mix 1¼ cups/300 ml of hand-hot water with the honey and yeast, stirring to dissolve. Leave for a couple of minutes, until bubbles rise to the top, then pour into the flour. Mix first with a fork, then with your hands, until you have a sticky dough, and tip onto a floured board or work surface. Form the dough into a ball, then knead by hand, pulling and stretching the dough for a good 4 or 5 minutes. If you have a stand mixer with a dough hook, you can use it to get the dough to this point.

Lightly oil the bowl, then return the dough to it, cover with a kitchen towel or plastic wrap and set aside in a warm place for about an hour, until the dough has

**MAKES 1 GOOD-SIZED LOAF**

1⅔ cups/250 g rye flour

2 cups/250 g spelt flour

1 teaspoon fine sea salt

3 tablespoons runny honey

2½ teaspoons/7 g dried yeast

1¾ ounces/50 g seeds (I use poppy and sunflower)

1 tablespoon caraway seeds (optional)

CONTINUED

risen by half (it won't rise as much as a normal loaf because of the rye flour).

Remove the dough from the bowl, place on a lightly floured board and knead again, briefly, for just a minute or two, adding and kneading in the seeds as you go.

Shape the dough into a flat oval and put it on an oiled baking sheet. Cover with the kitchen towel again and leave to rise once more for 30 minutes or so, until it has risen by half again. Preheat your oven to 475°F/240°C (convection 450°F/230°C).

After 30 minutes, slash the top of the dough in a crisscross pattern with a sharp knife and scatter over the caraway seeds.

Half fill a deep baking dish with boiling water and place on the bottom of your oven. This will create steam as the loaf bakes and help give your bread a lovely crust and texture.

Bake the loaf in the oven for 30 to 35 minutes, until golden all over. Be really careful when you open the oven door, as some hot steam may come out. To check if your bread is ready, lift it up and give it a tap on the bottom. If it sounds hollow, like a drum, it's good to go. Cool on a rack so the bottom keeps its lovely crust.

# How to make tahini

I am in love with tahini; I think there are very few things that a spoonful of tahini doesn't improve. It has been almost canonized in my house, where I have a couple of different types on the go at any time. I use it in smoothies; on porridge and pancakes; in soups, dressings, and stews; and spread on toast topped with banana. I like the deep, nut butter–style sweetness and its toasted earthiness.

There are many different types of tahini out there, ranging from the more liquid, lighter, sweeter Middle Eastern ones made with hulled sesame seeds to the health-food-shop, deep brown, raw, unhulled kind.

My favorite tahini is made from toasted unhulled sesame seeds. Toasting sesame seeds actually makes them easier to digest, improves their flavor, and makes them sweeter.

Unhulled sesame seeds, like whole wheat, have their outer casing intact. This outer part holds quite a few of the nutrients, so see if you can search them out; though if you can't, the hulled whiter seeds will do fine. Black sesame seeds will work just the same here too, and make an amazing dark, rich tahini.

A note on sterilizing jars: rather than boiling jars to sterilize them, warm them in the oven while you are working. Heat the oven to 275°F/140°C (convection 250°F/120°C). The jars should be in there for 10 minutes minimum, but can stay in longer. This process eliminates boring boiling and washing. The hottest cycle on your dishwasher will do the trick too; just make sure you fill the jars while they are still quite hot.

This will make about 1 cup/200 to 250 g.

...........................................................................................................

If you like your sesame seeds roasted (they usually are in tahini) put 7 ounces/200 g of sesame seeds into a dry frying pan over medium heat, stirring them to prevent them from burning, until they are lightly toasted (not too dark) and fragrant; this will take about 5 minutes. Transfer the toasted sesame seeds to a large plate and let them cool completely.

Place the sesame seeds in a food processor. Process for 2 to 3 minutes, until the seeds form a crumbly paste. Add 2 tablespoons of mild olive oil (or other mild-flavored oil, such as grapeseed or untoasted sesame) and process for a couple of minutes more, scraping down the sides as necessary, until the mixture forms a thick and fairly smooth paste. For thinner tahini, add more oil 1 to 2 tablespoons at a time, and process until the desired consistency is reached. Season well with sea salt and pulse again.

Transfer the tahini to a sterilized jar or other airtight container. Store in the fridge for a month or longer. If the mixture separates, just stir it well.

# Three vibrant dips

These are three quick and easy dips that I keep in my fridge in rotation. They are great for boosting quick meals and for quickly slathering on sandwiches. But more than anything, these are what I snack on: I dip a cracker (see page 260) or a carrot into whichever of these happens to be in the fridge. With these in my kitchen, my 4 p.m. raid of the cookie jar is often avoided.

2 cloves garlic

7 ounces/200 g red lentils, rinsed

juice of ½ lemon

2 tablespoons tahini

a good pinch of dried chile

1 tablespoon olive oil

TO SERVE

2 tablespoons toasted sesame seeds

chopped herbs or cresses (I use baby amaranth)

### RED LENTIL AND LEMON HUMMUS

Bash the garlic and put it into a small pan with the rinsed lentils. Cover with cold water and cook the lentils until tender and mashable, then drain and remove the skins of the garlic. Purée until whipped and smooth, add all the other ingredients, and blend again. Top with the toasted seeds and the herbs.

1 (9-ounce/250-g) package of cooked vacuum-packed beets

4 medjool dates

2 tablespoons regular or coconut yogurt

a small bunch of dill

1 unwaxed lemon

1 tablespoon olive oil

sea salt and freshly ground pepper

a handful of toasted walnuts

### BEET, WALNUT, AND DATE DIP

Blend the beets, dates, yogurt, and half the bunch of dill with the zest and juice of the lemon and the oil, and season well with salt and pepper. Throw in the toasted walnuts and purée again, keeping a bit of texture if you like; I like mine smooth.

7 ounces/200 g frozen peas

a small bunch of cilantro

a small bunch of mint

1 to 2 green chiles

2 unwaxed limes

sea salt and freshly ground pepper

¾ ounce/20 g coconut cream

### INDIAN GREEN PEA DIP

Fill and boil a kettle of water and get your ingredients together. Cover the peas with boiling water and put aside for a few minutes. Finely chop the cilantro and mint and put into a bowl. Finely chop the green chiles and zest both limes, and add both to the bowl, along with the juice of one of the limes. Season well with salt and pepper. Drain the peas and mash well, then add them to the herbs. Grate over the coconut cream and mix well.

# Amazing crackers

These easy crackers are perfectly snappable and are loaded with seeds and goodness. They are naturally wheat-free and can easily be gluten-free too if you use gluten-free oats. I keep a tin of these on hand for snacks and dipping. They last for ages and are really good for little people too—just leave the salt (and chile) out.

Most often I make these straight up with sea salt, but I have given a couple of flavoring options, one super savory and one sweet. Pretty much any dry spice would work here, so experiment with your favorites.

..................................................................................................................

Preheat your oven to 375°F/190°C (convection 350°F/175°C). Get all your ingredients together, and line two baking sheets with parchment paper.

Combine all the dry ingredients, including one of the optional flavorings if you are using them, and stir well. Mix the maple syrup, coconut oil, and water together in a measuring cup. Add to the dry ingredients and mix very well, until everything is completely soaked and the mixture becomes very thick.

Divide between the two lined sheets and even out a bit, then put another piece of parchment on top. Use a rolling pin to roll out the mixture until it is about ⅕ inch/½ cm thick. Take the top layer of parchment off and use the tip of a sharp knife to score the mixture into rectangles.

Bake the crackers for 20 minutes. Remove from the oven and flip the sheet over, then peel off the parchment to expose the underside of the crackers. Put back into the oven for another 20 minutes. They are ready when they are firm and golden round the edges.

Allow to cool, then break along the lines where they have been scored.

MAKES ENOUGH FOR 1 WEEK'S SNACKING

⅔ cup/100 g sunflower seeds
1½ cups/100 g pumpkin seeds
⅔ cup/100 g sesame seeds
6 tablespoons/50 g poppy seeds
⅓ cup/50 g chia seeds
2 cups/200 g rolled oats
1 teaspoon sea salt
1 tablespoon maple syrup
3 tablespoons melted coconut oil
1½ cups/350 ml water

OPTIONAL FLAVORINGS
1 heaping teaspoon fennel seeds and a pinch of dried chile
or
1 tablespoon raisins, coarsely chopped, and a pinch of cinnamon

# Coconut yogurt

This recipe requires some patience, but it's much cheaper than buying coconut milk yogurt, which is super expensive. Use the best pure coconut cream you can get, organic if possible.

Probiotics help your gut. You can use a container of plain yogurt in place of the capsules if you are not going for something dairy free.

..................................................................................

First, sterilize your jars. I do this by putting them through the hottest cycle of my dishwasher or into the oven at 350°F/170°C (convection 300°F/150°C) for about 20 minutes.

Place the coconut cream, still in its plastic wrapper, into a bowl of hot water to soften for 10 to 15 minutes. Massage the coconut with your hands to get rid of any lumps then squeeze out into a bowl. Whisk 1½ cups/350 ml of boiling water into the coconut cream, taking care to whisk out any lumps. Once it has cooled enough to touch, stir in the powder from the probiotic capsules and transfer to a jar.

If the weather is warm, leave the yogurt in a warm spot in the house for 12 to 24 hours. Otherwise you can put it into the oven at the lowest possible temperature for 8 to 10 hours.

Chill the yogurt for at least an hour, until it has cooled and has begun to thicken. It will thicken more as it is stored in the fridge, where it will keep for about 10 days.

**MAKES 2 GOOD-SIZED JARS**

1 (7-ounce/200-g) block of full-fat coconut cream
2 probiotic capsules

# Homemade milks from nuts, oats, and seeds

I have up to four different types of milk in my fridge at any one time, usually a small carton of organic milk, almond milk, oat milk, and, often, drinking coconut milk. I like to vary the kinds of milk I use, to make sure I am getting as much nutrition as possible and to make the most of the flavors of each individual milk: almond milk for coffee and baking, oat milk for hot chocolate, coconut milk for granola, and a jot of organic cow's milk for tea.

It is easy, more nutritious, and much cheaper to make your own nondairy milk at home. All you need is a decent blender and a nut milk bag (a muslin bag made for draining nut milk) or, failing that, a piece of muslin or a fine, thin kitchen towel.

These milks can be made from most nuts and seeds, and some grains. My favorites are almonds, pistachios, walnuts, hazelnuts, macadamia nuts, cashew nuts, sunflower seeds, pumpkin seeds, sesame seeds, hemp seeds, and oats. Opposite is a universal recipe that can be used for any of these. Since the formula works on ratios of volume rather than of weight, I have only included volume measures.

I have also included some of my favorite flavored milks, which I make from time to time to mix things up a bit.

### EASY HOMEMADE NUT MILK

Take 1 cup/250 ml of your chosen raw nut and place in a bowl. Cover with a cup of cold (ideally filtered) water and leave to soak for 8 hours; this will allow the nut to release all its nutrients and maximize the goodness in your milk.

Once the soaking time is up, drain the nuts and place in a blender, discarding the soaking water. Add 4 cups/1 liter of fresh cold (ideally filtered) water to the blender and blend until you have a thin, smooth, cloudy mixture.

Put a muslin bag or cloth over the mouth of a jug or pitcher and pour the nut milk through. Allow it to sit and drip into the jug for 5 to 10 minutes, then use your hands to squeeze out as much moisture from the nuts as you can.

Pour the milk into a clean bottle; it will keep in the fridge for 3 to 4 days. The leftover nut pulp can be added to hummus or can be used in place of ground almonds in baking.

### ALMOND, TURMERIC, AND HONEY MILK

Follow the recipe at left, using almonds. Before blending, add a pinch of ground turmeric, a pinch of ground cardamom, and a tablespoon of honey to make a beautiful yellow milk.

### SESAME, DATE, AND CINNAMON MILK

Use sesame seeds to make your milk, and before blending add 4 pitted medjool dates and a pinch of cinnamon.

### OAT AND MAPLE MILK

Use 1/2 cup/125 g each of oats and pecans to make your milk and add 1 to 2 tablespoons of maple syrup before blending.

### LEMON ZEST AND VANILLA MILK

Use pistachios to make your milk and add the zest of 1/2 lemon and a drop of vanilla extract before blending.

# Rainbow paletas

All over Mexico, there are shops dedicated to Mexican frozen pops called *paletas*. These shops are filled with a few deep glass-topped chest freezers, where a rainbow of cheery *paletas* line up as in a frozen sweet shop. They come packed with just about anything you can think of—strawberry, mango, guava, avocado, pineapple, watermelon, and horchata were my highlights when I was there, most in almost neon brilliance. I must have eaten at least one a day. The Mexican ones are made with barely smashed fruit and lots of sugar.

These are my version, all good stuff and a bit of natural sweetness packed into a frozen pop so you always have a nourishing sweet treat at your fingertips.

I encourage you to taste the mixtures before you freeze them to check for balance, sweetness, and sourness. Do remember that they will taste subtler and less sweet once frozen.

2 ripe avocados
1¼ cups/300 ml coconut water
juice of 1 lemon
seeds from a vanilla pod, or 1 teaspoon vanilla paste
1 teaspoon runny honey

### AVOCADO, HONEY, VANILLA
Pit the avocados and scoop the flesh into a blender. Add all the other ingredients and blend until smooth. Taste for sweetness and add a little more honey if needed. Pour into molds and freeze for at least 4 hours.

10 ounces/300 g cucumber
a bunch of mint
½ cup/100 ml elderflower cordial
zest and juice of 2 unwaxed limes
a small swig of gin (optional)

### ELDERFLOWER, CUCUMBER, LIME
Put the peeled and coarsely chopped cucumber and the leaves from the mint into a blender and blend for a few seconds, so that a little texture remains. Pour into a bowl and add the cordial, lime zest and juice, and, if you like, a good swig of gin. Taste and adjust the lime or sweetness if needed. Pour into molds and freeze for at least 4 hours.

CONTINUED

1½ cups/350 ml unsweetened almond milk
6 dates
seeds from a vanilla pod, or 1 teaspoon vanilla paste
2 tablespoons maple syrup

**DATE, ALMOND MILK, MAPLE**
Put all the ingredients into a blender and blend until the dates are well puréed. Pour into molds and freeze for at least 4 hours.

7 ounces/200 g strawberries
3 tablespoons/50 ml agave syrup
½ cup/100 ml coconut water
zest and juice of 1 unwaxed lemon
½ teaspoon fennel seeds, bashed

**STRAWBERRY, LEMON, FENNEL SEED**
Hull the strawberries and put them into a blender. Blend until you have a rough purée, then tip into a bowl and mix in the agave syrup, coconut water, lemon zest and juice, and the bashed fennel seeds. Pour into molds and freeze for at least 4 hours.

# Carrot cake granola bars

I'm not sure what my favorite cake is. It's a toss-up between a lemon drizzle, a carrot cake, and my ginger, molasses, and apple cake, but it's safe to say carrot cake always makes the top three. Here I've brought together carrot cake and another favorite thing, flapjacks. The first time I made granola bars I was open-mouthed as I mixed so much butter and sugar into the oats. A lot of my friends still eat them, thinking they are a healthy treat; a few oats will fool anyone. These little squares, however, are sweetened with some dried fruit and maple syrup, and, as sweet things go, they are fairly virtuous.

Sometimes I mix up the spices here and use a little cardamom in place of the cinnamon.

.......................................................................................................

Preheat the oven to 400°F/200°C (convection 350°F/180°C). Get all your ingredients together. Soak the chia seeds in 4 tablespoons of water in a little bowl. Melt the coconut oil.

Line an 9 by 13–inch/20 by 30–cm baking dish with parchment paper. Put the oats into a food processor and pulse until you have a scruffy flour, then tip the oat flour into a large mixing bowl.

Put half the dried fruit into the food processor and process until it is broken down and a little mushy. Scrape into the bowl with the oats.

Peel and grate the carrot and the apple (no need to peel) into the large mixing bowl and add the coconut, chia mixture, pumpkin seeds, maple syrup, vanilla, spices, and melted coconut oil. Mix well.

Spoon onto the lined baking dish, smooth over the top with the back of a spoon, and bake for 40 to 45 minutes, until golden brown. Allow to cool a little on the dish, then completely on a rack, and slice into 16 pieces.

MAKES 16 BARS

4 tablespoons chia seeds

1¾ ounces/50 g coconut oil

2 cups/200 g rolled oats

5 ounces/150 g dried fruit (I use a mixture of dried apricots and raisins)

1 medium carrot

1 apple

3½ ounces/100 g desiccated coconut

3½ ounces/100 g pumpkin seeds

4 tablespoons maple syrup

1 tablespoon vanilla extract

½ teaspoon ground cinnamon

a pinch of ground ginger

# Summer rhubarb
# and strawberry crisp bars

Just-right, sweet yet tart, scarlet and vibrant pink summer fruit sits on top of a half-pastry, half-granola base, all topped off with a crunchy crumble topping. These bars are free from eggs, dairy, and refined sugar, and are gluten-free if you use a gluten-free flour blend.

If coconut sugar and oil are too much of a stretch for you, follow the recipe using the same quantities of butter and soft light brown sugar. You can vary the fruits you use here depending on the time of year: apples and blackberries are great, as are plums and pears. In the summer, apricots and raspberries are amazing.

Preheat the oven to 400°F/210°C (convection 375°F/ 190°C) and get all your ingredients and equipment together. Line an 9 by 13–inch/20 by 30–cm baking dish with parchment paper and rub with a little coconut oil.

Put the coconut oil or butter into a large saucepan over medium heat and leave to melt, then take off the heat. Add the oats, flour, 1 cup/150 g of sugar, and a pinch of salt and give it a good mix. Take out 6 tablespoons of the mixture and put to one side to make the topping. Using the back of a spoon, press the rest of the mixture into the bottom of the baking dish until it evenly coats the dish.

Chop the rhubarb and the strawberries quite finely and put into a bowl. Squeeze over the lemon juice, add the remaining 1 tablespoon of sugar, and toss to coat. Scatter the fruit over the crumb base then sprinkle with the reserved topping. Bake for 40 minutes, until the fruit is bubbly and the crumbs are golden.

Let the bars cool in the tray (you can do this in the fridge to speed things up), then cut into about 20 pieces. These will keep for 4 to 5 days in the fridge.

MAKES ABOUT 20 BARS

5 ounces/150 g coconut oil or butter, plus extra for greasing

1½ cups/150 g rolled oats

1¼ cups/150 g spelt flour

1 cup/150 g coconut sugar or unrefined light brown sugar, plus 1 tablespoon

9 ounces/250 g rhubarb (about 2 medium stalks)

10 ounces/300 g strawberries, hulled

juice of 1 lemon

# Amazing lemon cannellini cake

A cake made of beans? I thought it sounded absolutely ridiculous too. But I gave it a try anyway, and when a springy, light, well-crumbed sponge appeared 30 minutes later, it was a revelation.

This cake is pretty great. It's totally grain-, gluten-, refined sugar-, and dairy-free and it tastes as indulgent and amazing as any cake should.

I made a candied lemon topping. It's pretty easy, but if you don't have the time or the inclination, a good grating of lemon zest will do. To make the candied lemon peel, peel the zest off a lemon, drop it into boiling water for a couple of minutes, then transfer to a pan and add a couple of tablespoons of maple syrup. Place over high heat for a couple of minutes, until the peel becomes translucent. Transfer to a parchment-lined plate and don't touch until it's cool.

...............................................................................

Preheat the oven to 375°F/190°C (convection 350°F/180°C) and get all your ingredients together. Grease an 8-inch/20-cm springform cake pan and line the bottom and sides with parchment paper. Drain the cannellini beans.

In a food processor, purée the drained beans, honey, and vanilla seeds until smooth, then add the eggs one by one, pulsing as you go. Tip the whole lot into a mixing bowl and gently fold in the ground almonds, baking powder, melted coconut oil, and salt. The batter may be a little looser than you'd expect from a cake batter, but don't worry.

Pour the mixture into the prepared pan and bake for 30 to 40 minutes. The cake is ready when it is golden

:·:· CONTINUED

SERVES 8 TO 10

FOR THE CAKE

2 (14-ounce/400-g) cans of cannellini beans
⅔ cup/150 ml semisolidified honey
seeds from 1 vanilla pod
4 free-range or organic eggs
3½ ounces/100 g ground almonds
2 teaspoons gluten-free baking powder
3½ ounces/100 g melted coconut oil
a good pinch of sea salt

FOR THE LEMON ICING

7 ounces/200 g silken tofu
2 tablespoons melted coconut oil
zest and juice of 1 unwaxed lemon
2 tablespoons semisolidified honey
1 teaspoon orange blossom water

brown on top and firm to the touch and a skewer comes out clean.

For the icing, put all the ingredients into a blender and blend until very smooth and shiny, scraping down the sides from time to time if you need to. This will take 3 to 4 minutes. Transfer to a bowl and pop into the fridge to set while the cake is cooking and cooling.

Once the cake has had its time, take it out of the oven, leave it to cool for 5 minutes in the pan, then cool completely on a rack.

Once the cake is cool, top with the icing and either grate over more lemon zest or finish with the candied lemon (see headnote).

# Sweet potato and malted chocolate cake

I think every cook needs a good chocolate cake up their sleeve. I have spent years chasing my dream chocolate cake, and for the time being this is it. A double-layered, light-as-a-feather chocolate sponge, sandwiched with a foolproof icing.

I use sweet potato here to add natural sweetness and for a moist but perfectly light and bouncy well-crumbed cake. The sweet potato means that you need less sugar and less butter, but there is no compromise on flavor.

The icing is based on the famous Brooklyn blackout cake, though mine is a good bit less heavy-duty than the original. You cook the icing like a custard, which makes it really easy to work with when cool and amazingly glossy and rich, like a chocolate ganache but without being loaded with cream.

....................................................................................................

Preheat the oven to 400°F/200°C (convection 350°F/180°C) and get all your ingredients together. Grease two 8-inch/20-cm springform pans and line the bottoms with parchment paper.

First, make the sweet potato purée. Peel and coarsely chop the sweet potatoes, then steam or boil them until cooked. Drain, reserving the cooking water, then purée them in a blender or mash them really well until smooth, adding about 4 tablespoons of the cooking water to loosen a little.

Sift the flour, ground cinnamon, cocoa, baking powder, and salt into a bowl. In a separate bowl, mix together the sweet potato mash and the yogurt.

SERVES 10 TO 12

7 ounces/200 g sweet potatoes
2¼ cups/275 g spelt flour
½ teaspoon ground cinnamon
4 tablespoons good-quality cocoa powder
2 teaspoons baking powder
a pinch of fine sea salt
⅓ cup/100 g Greek yogurt
5 ounces/150 g butter or coconut oil, at room temperature
5 ounces/150 g soft light brown sugar or coconut sugar
1 teaspoon vanilla extract
3 large free-range or organic eggs

FOR THE CHOCOLATE CUSTARD ICING
⅓ cup/75 g cornstarch
2½ cups/600 ml unsweetened almond milk
1½ cups/300 g golden superfine sugar or coconut sugar
2 tablespoons barley malt extract
1 cup/100 g good-quality cocoa powder, sifted
1 teaspoon vanilla extract

⋰ CONTINUED

Using a stand mixer or a bowl with a handheld electric mixer, cream together the butter and sugar until pale and fluffy. Stop occasionally to scrape the mixture off the side of the bowl with a spatula. Add the vanilla, then mix in the eggs one by one. Add the dry ingredients and slowly mix until just combined—don't overwork it. Fold in the sweet potato and yogurt mixture, then divide evenly between the two lined pans. Bake on the middle shelf of the oven for around 35 minutes, until cooked through—a skewer inserted into the center of the cake should come out clean. Leave the sponges to cool in the pans for 5 minutes, then transfer them to a rack to cool completely.

Meanwhile, make your chocolate icing. Blend the cornstarch with about a third of the almond milk, until smooth. Bring the remaining almond milk to a boil in a small nonstick saucepan with the sugar, barley malt, and cocoa, whisking until smooth. Add the cornstarch mixture and bring to a boil, stirring constantly, until you have a rich, thick custard. Remove from the heat, add the vanilla extract, and stir well. Ideally the mixture should be silky smooth, but if not, give it a quick whiz in a food processor. Pour into a large bowl, cover the surface with plastic wrap and put into the fridge to cool completely.

To assemble, cut each of the cakes in half and give the chocolate-custard filling a stir. Spread the filling over one of the cake layers, taking it almost to the rim, then place another cake layer on top and repeat until you have the four layers stacked, with the best-looking layer on top. Coat the top of the cake with the remaining custard icing and let it drizzle down the sides.

super-fast
breakfasts

Breakfast is my favorite meal and, for me, eating a good breakfast is how I set my intentions for the day. My mornings, like most people's, are rushed, but these breakfasts can be put together quickly, and there are a couple of slightly longer ones for the weekend: goodness-packed açai bowls, fluffy almond-milk French toast, easy favorite smoothies, 10-minute pancakes, avocado fritters, and quick but delicious porridge.

açai bowls · almond milk, ricotta, and lemon french toast · strawberry, coconut, and cardamom smoothie · morning smoothies · tahini-drizzled superfruit · 10-minute pancakes · nordic morning bowls · overnight oats · peach and raspberry ripple breakfast · avocado fritters · golden turmeric milk · red quinoa porridge

# Açai bowls

I ate these like they were going out of fashion one summer in Brazil, and they are still one of my favorite things to start the day with. In the healthy eating world, smoothie bowls have become quite a thing, but this is the original. It is eaten cold, which I don't mind in summer or in winter.

Açai berries have been called superfoods for the high levels of nutrients they contain. They are jam-packed with antioxidants, amino acids, and omega fatty acids. It can be pretty hard to come by them frozen, let alone fresh, so I've used açai powder here. Açai powder isn't the cheapest, but for the amount of nutrition it provides your body, I think it's a good investment. These bowls can be made with just the frozen berries if açai powder eludes you.

This recipe uses frozen bananas. Freezing bananas is a great way to make use of any that are going unloved in your fruit bowl. Make sure you peel them first. I cut mine into ¾-inch/2-cm chunks and put them into a sandwich bag; I then lay the filled and sealed bag flat in the freezer, spreading the banana pieces out so they don't stick together.

Get all your ingredients together.

Place the banana, berries, açai powder, honey, and most of the milk in a blender and blend until creamy and smooth, adding more milk to thin the mixture if needed. Aim for a thick, almost ice cream–like consistency. If you don't have a regular blender, a good handheld blender, a jug, and a bit of determination will work fine.

Spoon the açai mixture into bowls, top with your choice of toppings, and pretend you are on Ipanema Beach.

**MAKES 2 BOWLS**

1 large banana (frozen if possible—see headnote)

7 ounces/200 g fresh or frozen berries (2 handfuls)

3 tablespoons açai powder

1 teaspoon runny honey

scant ½ cup/100 ml your choice of milk (I use unsweetened almond)

**TOP WITH ANY OF THE FOLLOWING**

granola

seeds (I use hemp and pumpkin)

bee pollen

goji berries

chopped almonds

desiccated coconut

honey

nut butter

# Almond milk, ricotta, and lemon French toast

This is the quickest and most indulgent breakfast I know. It's usually saved for weekends as it's more substantial than my weekday breakfast, but it's easily quick enough for a weekday.

I love the simple flavors here: vanilla, lemon, and creamy ricotta. I like to use good sheep's milk ricotta if I can get my hands on it. The rest of the container is great stirred through pasta or spread on toast and topped with berries.

I have found that decent gluten-free bread works really well too, as the almond milk mixture helps prevent the bread from being too dry. Vegans you can make the French toast with extra almond milk and skip the eggs and use some coconut yogurt in place of the ricotta.

Get all your ingredients and equipment together.

Break the eggs into a bowl and whisk in the almond milk and vanilla. Pour into a deep baking dish and lay all four slices of bread in the mixture. Leave to soak for a minute.

Put a pan over medium heat and add a good dollop of coconut oil or butter. Turn the bread over and leave for another minute to soak up the mixture, then carefully lower into the pan and cook for 2 to 3 minutes on each side until golden and crisp, taking care when you flip it, as the bread will be quite delicate.

Pile two slices on each plate, dot with ricotta, and grate over the zest of the lemon. Top with honey, if you like things sweet.

**SERVES 2**

2 free-range or organic eggs

½ cup/125 ml unsweetened almond milk

seeds from 1 vanilla pod, or 1 teaspoon vanilla paste

4 thick slices of good bread or brioche

coconut oil or butter

2 tablespoons good ricotta cheese

1 unwaxed lemon

runny honey and berry compote, to serve (optional)

# Strawberry, coconut, and cardamom smoothie

This smoothie is bliss. It is comforting, refreshing, and nourishing all at once. I often find green smoothies or juices a bit hard to handle in the morning. I crave something milky. I first made this drink one summer in California, and I think I must have had it for breakfast every day for the following two weeks. The coconut and almonds mean it's packed with protein and good fats.

I love the depth the cardamom brings, but if you are not a fan, a pinch of ground cinnamon will work well too.

It's important to note that the coconut milk I use for this smoothie is the stuff for pouring over your cereal, not the stuff in a can, which would be too rich and thick. Coconut water also works well.

**MAKES 1 LARGE BREAKFAST GLASS OR 2 SMALLER ONES**

4 tablespoons desiccated coconut

a handful of strawberries or frozen berries

⅞ cup/200 ml drinking coconut milk or almond milk

a small handful of almonds

seeds from 1 cardamom pod

1 teaspoon light agave syrup or runny honey

Put all the ingredients into a blender and blend until smooth and frothy. You will need a good blender to pulverize the coconut and almonds completely. If yours is less powerful, blend for longer until it is completely smooth. If your smoothie looks too thick, add a little ice-cold water bit by bit until you have the consistency you like. Pour into a tall glass or two smaller ones.

# morning smoothies

Smoothies are my favorite way of getting goodness into my body when time is short. If you are really bad in the mornings (like me), you can prep the jar of ingredients the night before and leave it in the fridge overnight. I've left quantities a little vague here, as you will want to tweak to your taste. You can make these smoothies a bit thicker and serve them in a bowl topped with fruit or add-ons (see below). In the winter, frozen fruits are always in my freezer; they are cheaper than fresh, they taste great, and they make lovely thick smoothies. I like my smoothies with a little ice—though not too cold. You can't go wrong if you follow this template.

**CREAMY FRUIT**
Banana, avocado
(40 percent)

|

**BACK-UP FRUIT OR VEGETABLE**
Strawberries, apples, spinach
(20 percent)

|

**FLAVORING**
Vanilla, lemon, tahini
(spoonful)

|

**SWEETNESS**
Chopped date, maple syrup,
honey (dash)

|

**PROTEIN BOOST**
Soaked seeds, soaked nuts, protein
powder, nut butter
(tablespoon)

|

**LIQUID**
Nut milk, coconut water
(40 percent)

**FAVORITE ADD-ONS**

**LUCUMA**   This superfruit from Peru is high in antioxidants and minerals and beta-carotene.

**MACA**   This comes in a powdered form and is thought to calm the nervous system and help our bodies cope with stress. Look for 100 percent maca root when you are buying it.

**HEMP**   This comes in seed and powder form and is one of the only complete plant sources of protein. It is also high in omega-3 and omega-6 and in fiber.

**BEE POLLEN**   This is an incredible whole food providing almost every nutrient, mineral, and vitamin our bodies need. It is powerful stuff, so start with just a teaspoon a day.

**SPIRULINA AND CHLORELLA**   These are two types of algae, which are insanely rich in protein and nutrients. This stuff is like a natural green caffeine.

## FAVORITE SMOOTHIES

### MANGO SESAME

boosts calcium, anti-inflammatory

Frozen banana · Mango or persimmon ·
Turmeric · Tahini or sesame seeds ·
Lime · Almond milk

### CHOCOLATE SHAKE

Frozen banana · Avocado · Cacao ·
Maple syrup · Plant milk

### GINGER PEAR REFRESHER

Avocado · Green apple or pear ·
Celery · Mint · Ginger · Coconut water

### CARROT AND GINGER

high in vitamin C, antiviral

Frozen banana · Apple or carrot ·
Orange · Lemon · Ginger · Plant milk

### MAGENTA

Strawberries · Raw beet ·
Pomegranate · Ginger · Dates ·
Coconut water

### GOOD GREENS

electrolytes, protein;
good after workout

Frozen banana · Avocado · Celery
· Kiwi · Hemp seeds · Almonds ·
Coconut water

### STONE FRUIT

Peach · Apricot · Plum · Berries ·
Vanilla extract · Açai · Plant milk

### LEMON VANILLA, LAYERED

vitamin C, antibacterial,
aids digestion

**Bottom layer** · Raspberries and
maple syrup; blend and pour into
glass · **Top layer** · Frozen bananas
· Vanilla extract · Zest of ½ lemon ·
Honey · Coconut milk

### PEANUT BUTTER AND STRAWBERRY, LAYERED

**Bottom layer** · Strawberries, lime
juice, and honey; blend and pour
into glass · **Top layer** · Banana ·
Vanilla extract · Peanut butter ·
Plant milk

# Tahini-drizzled superfruit

SERVES 2

FOR THE TAHINI DRESSING

4 tablespoons tahini

2 to 4 tablespoons runny honey, to taste

juice of 1 lemon

a good pinch of ground cinnamon

FOR THE FRUITS

2 bowls of seasonal fruits:

spring—Alphonso mango, blood oranges, strawberries

summer—raspberries, peaches, apricots, cherries

autumn—pears, plums, blackberries, figs, blueberries

winter—apples, pears, persimmons, pomegranates

2 tablespoons seeds (hemp, sesame, and sunflower work well)

2 tablespoons goji berries or raisins

Having the same thing every morning seems a waste of a golden opportunity. I like to mix up what I have for breakfast just as I would my lunch or dinner. And breakfast has to start me off on the right foot: bright-colored food packed with goodness, but it has to fill me up or I get grumpy.

This is what I make when I want a bowl of fruit. It is a true fruit salad in that it even has a dressing. The dressing sweetens the fruit a little, which I love, as sometimes I find it too acidic to eat first thing, and it also adds a kick of morning protein.

If you are a tahini lover like me, give this a try. If you are less convinced about tahini you could swap it for almond butter for a more mellow dressing.

Get all your ingredients together.

Put the dressing ingredients and a couple of tablespoons of cold water into a jar with a screwtop lid and shake until well combined.

Wash and chop the fruit and arrange in bowls. Top each bowl with a spoonful of seeds and berries and drizzle with the tahini dressing.

# 10-minute pancakes

These are a fast-forward version of my favorite-ever pancakes. This time the whole process is done in a blender, but if you don't have one, you can make these with oat flour instead of oats and ground almonds instead of whole nuts, and mash the banana well.

I use a teacup for measuring to save time in the mornings. The pancakes may vary a little from cup to cup but it's really the ratio that makes this recipe work, so don't worry.

Since they are sweetened with natural nutrient-rich bananas and maple syrup and use whole grains instead of flour, you can happily eat these pancakes with gusto.

Get all your ingredients and equipment together.

Put the oats into a blender and blend until you have a scruffy flour. Grate the apple. Put the nuts, milk, apple, and banana into the blender and blend until combined.

Heat a nonstick pan over medium heat and add a little coconut oil or butter. Allow it to melt, then add ladlefuls of the pancake batter to make small pancake rounds. Cook for 2 to 3 minutes, or until bubbles rise to the surface. Use a spatula to carefully flip the pancakes over and cook on the other side. The pancakes in the first batch are always more delicate, so don't worry if they look a bit scruffy. Keep them warm while you cook the rest.

Once all your pancakes are done, use a Y peeler to peel your apples into long pieces then put into a bowl and toss with the lemon juice, cinnamon, and nutmeg.

Serve the pancakes stacked and topped with the apple strips, maple syrup, and, if you like, a little yogurt.

## MAKES 6 PANCAKES

¾ cup/80 g oats

1 apple

a good handful of nuts (about 1¾ ounces/50 g)— pecans or almonds

⅔ cup/150 ml milk of your choice (I use unsweetened almond)

1 medium banana

coconut oil or butter

## TO FINISH

2 apples

juice of ½ lemon

a pinch of cinnamon

a tiny grating of nutmeg

maple syrup or honey

yogurt of your choice (I use coconut) (optional)

# Nordic morning bowls

I have come to think of porridge in the same way I think of soup—as a wonderful warming bowl of gentle goodness—but that's not enough for me. I like texture changes and flavor pops in my food, so just as I spend a few extra minutes thinking about how to create toppings, texture, and flavor for a bowl of soup, I have started to do the same for my bowls of porridge.

I tend to eat porridge when it's cold, so Nordic spices and wintry vibes are what I want.

If you can think ahead, putting the oats, milk, and spices into a bowl and then into the fridge overnight will help make the oats easier to digest and save you time in the morning. Just pour into a pan when you're ready to make your porridge. This works well with quinoa flakes or millet flakes too.

Get all your ingredients and equipment together.

Put the oats and milk into a saucepan with ½ cup/125 ml of cold water and a pinch of salt and start to warm it over medium heat. Pit and coarsely chop the dates and add to the pan with all the spices and the vanilla.

Stir the porridge and cook until it is thick and creamy. Once you've got it to the consistency you like, take it off the heat and spoon it into deep bowls, adding a squeeze of honey if you like your porridge sweet. Top with a spoonful of almond butter, a scattering of raisins and hemp seeds, a spoonful of coconut yogurt, and a good grating of apple. Hand-warming bowls of good stuff.

SERVES 4

2 cups/200 g rolled oats

1¼ cups/300 ml milk of your choice
(I use unsweetened almond)

2 dates

sea salt

a pinch of ground cinnamon

a pinch of freshly grated nutmeg

a pinch of ground cardamom

1 teaspoon vanilla extract

TO TOP

honey (optional)

2 tablespoons almond butter

a handful of raisins or currants

a scattering of hemp seeds

coconut yogurt

1 apple

# overnight oats

Overnight oats are what I often make when
I know my morning will be rushed. They are so
easy, and take 2 minutes to throw together the
night before. I find them particularly useful when
I'm going on a long journey or traveling. If you
are grabbing them to take to work or on a plane
or train, mix them in a screw-top jar so they are
ready to go. Frozen fruits work well here, as they
are cheaper than fresh and defrost in the fridge
overnight. For all these recipes, follow the ratio
below for 2 servings, mix all the ingredients
in a bowl or jar, and leave in the fridge overnight.

- **GRAIN (1 CUP/100 G)** • oats, rye flakes, quinoa flakes

- **LIQUID (SCANT 1½ CUPS/330 ML)** • plant milk, water, coconut milk

- **SEEDS (2 TABLESPOONS)** • pumpkin, flax, chia

- **SWEETNESS (DASH)** • maple syrup, vanilla

• oats • coconut milk • chia • desiccated coconut, honey, mango

• oats • almond milk • chia • vanilla, strawberries

• oats • plant milk • chia • bashed cardamom, honey, raspberries, lemon zest

• quinoa flakes • nut milk • chia • lemon zest, berries

• oats • plant milk • banana, raisins, almonds, peanut butter

• buckwheat groats • plant milk • hemp • figs, apple, cinnamon

• oats • almond milk • chia • maple syrup

• oats • vanilla, dates, figs, nutmeg, maple syrup, cinnamon

• oats • nut milk • flax • vanilla, plums, maple syrup

• oats • chia • vanilla, lemon, peaches, maple syrup

# Peach and raspberry ripple breakfast

This breakfast is a quick one, but it does call for you to soak the oats overnight so they're soft enough to blend. It's really easy—I am not super-organized and I don't remember to do this all the time, but when I do, it feels satisfying.

I eat this cold, and for me it's a summer alternative to porridge, which I only really eat on the coldest days of the year. If you like, you can warm it a little, though it does lose some of its raw credentials.

This recipe is inspired by one on one of my favorite blogs, *My New Roots*, by Sarah Britton, who was flying the flag for inspired plant-based eating long before it was so mainstream. Sarah uses buckwheat instead of oats, which is also delicious. She also inspired me to swirl my breakfast like raspberry ripple ice cream or a 1980s dessert plate.

SERVES 3 TO 4

1 cup/100 g oats
juice of ½ lemon or 1 teaspoon apple cider vinegar
2 tablespoons chia seeds
½ cup/125 ml milk of your choice, or water
1 frozen banana
1 vanilla pod, seeds scraped

FOR THE RASPBERRY AND PEACH RIPPLE
7 ounces/200 g raspberries (fresh or frozen, organic if possible)
1 peach
1 tablespoon maple syrup (optional)

Get all your ingredients together. Cover the oats with warm water and the lemon juice or vinegar and let it sit overnight. Next morning, drain the oats and rinse very well.

In a regular blender, food processor, or high-speed blender (this works the best), blend the raspberries, peach flesh, and maple syrup until they are liquid. Spoon out about half into a bowl and set aside.

Leave the remaining purée in the blender and add the drained and rinsed oats and the rest of the ingredients. Blend on the highest setting until it's really smooth and silky. Taste and add a little maple syrup if you like things sweeter.

Serve the porridge in bowls or little glasses, with the raspberry and peach purée swirled in. Leftovers keep in the fridge for up to 2 days.

# Avocado fritters

These cloudlike bright green fritters are polenta-crusted and, if you are an avocado fan, I think you should run into the kitchen and make them right away. I thought I'd had avocado in every way possible until I ate these. My dear friend Emily and I whipped them up one morning while trying out recipes for this book.

I top these vivid fritters with a quick cashew hollandaise and sometimes a poached egg, but I leave the egg out if I'm making this for my vegan brother and sister, and they love it just as much.

These are a great way to use avocados that are a little overripe, and a brilliant way to use up cooked quinoa. I always have some cooked quinoa in the freezer (see pages 246–247), which makes this even faster.

................................................................................................

Fill and boil a kettle of water and get all your ingredients and equipment together. Put the cashews into a heatproof bowl and cover with boiling water from the kettle.

If you need to, cook your quinoa. Measure it out in a mug or measuring cup, making a note of the level it comes to, rinse well in cold water, then pour it into a large saucepan. Fill the mug to the same level with boiling water and add to the pan, then repeat so you have double the volume of water as quinoa. Cook for 10 to 12 minutes, until translucent and the little curly grains have popped out. Drain well and leave to cool slightly.

While the quinoa is cooking, get on with some other jobs. Peel and pit the avocados, then mash coarsely, still leaving some texture and a few lumps. Grate over the zest of 1 lime, then squeeze in the juice and mix well.

CONTINUED

## SERVES 4

### FOR THE FRITTERS
½ cup/75 g quinoa
(or 1 cup/150 g cooked)
4 avocados
1 unwaxed lime
3½ ounces/100 g kale
1 green chile
a bunch of cilantro
sea salt and freshly ground pepper
1 cup/150 g polenta
coconut oil
4 free-range or organic eggs
(optional)

### FOR THE HOLLANDAISE
5 ounces/150 g cashews
½ teaspoon ground turmeric
juice of 1 lime
1 tablespoon olive oil
sea salt

Wash the kale, then tear off and discard the stalks. Tear the leaves into small pieces. Finely chop the green chile, then cut the stalks off the bunch of cilantro and finely chop the leaves.

Add the kale, chile, and cilantro to the bowl of avocado, along with the cooked and drained quinoa and a good pinch of salt and pepper, and mix well.

Divide the mixture into eight and shape into eight patties. Pour the polenta onto a baking dish and spread it out into one thick layer. One by one, lay each fritter on top then sprinkle some polenta from the tray generously over the other side. Pop into the fridge to set while you make the hollandaise.

Drain the soaked cashews, mix the turmeric with 3 tablespoons of hot water, then put both into a food processor with the lime juice, oil, and a good pinch of salt. Blitz until smooth and glossy—this will take a little longer if your blender is not a high-speed one. You can also use a handheld blender.

Heat a pan over medium heat, add a little coconut oil, and fry the patties until golden on both sides. You can either use two pans here or you can fry in batches, keeping the cooked fritters warm in a low oven.

If you are topping your fritters with a poached egg, now is the time to poach the eggs, while the fritters are frying. Everyone has their own method— I drop the eggs into a just-simmering shallow pan of water for 3 to 4 minutes, depending on the temperature of the eggs and how runny I want them.

Serve two fritters each, with a poached egg if that's your thing, and plenty of hollandaise. Serve to smiling faces at the table.

# Golden turmeric milk

I am a hot-drink person. I love tea in all its forms: Earl Grey in the morning, fennel, rose, cinnamon, chamomile, you name it. The work surface next to my kettle is piled high with jars of petals and flowers from far-flung places, caddies of tea, and carefully chosen occasional coffee. But when the nights draw in, I like something more comforting, and this is my new blanket of a drink.

Its sunny yellow color brightens up my mornings. The spices calm and soothe my bedtimes. I try to have a little turmeric every day, usually in a tea, because its healing and anticancer properties have been widely celebrated. I love its saffron-toned vibrancy and its like-nothing-else taste, so it's not a hardship by any means.

I prefer not to have too much dairy, especially before bed, so I make this with unsweetened oat or coconut milk. I make a peppy morning version with a little bashed ginger in place of the cinnamon, too. Allowing the milk to cool a little before you add the honey will keep the heat from damaging the nutrients in the honey.

SERVES 1

2 cardamom pods
⅞ cup/200 ml unsweetened oat, coconut, almond, or any milk you like
¼ teaspoon ground turmeric
¼ teaspoon ground cinnamon
1 teaspoon runny honey

Bash the cardamom pods in a mortar with a pestle and put into a small saucepan with the milk, turmeric, and cinnamon. Heat gently until it is almost boiling, but don't let it boil; otherwise, if you are using a nondairy milk, your milk may split.

Pour into a mug (you can pour through a strainer if the cardamom seeds bother you) and, once it has cooled a little, stir in the honey and drink, making sure not to spill any, as its lovely yellow color can be rather staining.

# Red quinoa porridge

My sister Laura and I have always been joined at the hip. We have the same voice, mannerisms, and sense of humor and we chat every day, even though she lives on the other side of the world. While I was writing this book, my sister was camped out in Peru, overloading on her favorite food, quinoa, and buying piles of alpaca blankets she'll probably regret when she gets home. This porridge was inspired by a picture Laura sent me from a Peruvian café.

If you are avoiding gluten, you can leave out the oats here; they add a little creaminess to the porridge, so you may need to cook it for a little longer to get it really creamy without.

Here I top my porridge with mango, coconut, passionfruit, and lime, but you could vary the fruits and use whatever is in season. My favorites are:

> spring—poached apricots, saffron, pistachios
> summer—strawberries, vanilla, lemon
> autumn—plums, oranges, cinnamon
> winter—blood oranges, dates, pomegranates

SERVES 2

scant ⅔ cup/100 g red quinoa
(or white or black)
½ cup/50 g rolled oats
⅔ cup/150 ml unsweetened
almond milk
a pinch of cinnamon
2 dates

TO SERVE
1 mango
1 passionfruit
coconut yogurt
coconut flakes
1 unwaxed lime

Put the quinoa, oats, almond milk, and cinnamon into a pan with a scant ½ cup/100 ml of cold water and bring to a simmer over medium heat. Pit and chop the dates and add them to the pan for sweetness.

Cook for 10 minutes, until the quinoa has softened and cooked and the curly quinoa grains are visible. Make sure you stir every so often so it doesn't stick.

Meanwhile, peel and chop the mango and coarsely chop a few more dates. Once the porridge is cooked and is the consistency you like, spoon it into bowls, pile on the mango, dates, yogurt, and coconut flakes, and finish with a good grating of lime zest.

quick
desserts
and
sweet
treats

I love desserts and I often reach for something sweet midafternoon. These desserts and treats are made with unrefined sugars, oats, nuts, and seeds and the odd bit of chocolate. The desserts come together in minutes, while the treats take a little longer to make but will sit happily in a container to satisfy those sweet cravings throughout the week.

saffron apricots · raw cookie dough bars · coconut and goji fudge bites · rhubarb, apple, and maple pan crumble · chocolate and earl grey pudding pots · banana, date, and candied pecan ice cream · coconut, rhubarb, and lime panna cotta · salted almond butter chocolate bars · honey and orange ricotta and baked figs · cranachan · quick fruit desserts · dark chocolate goodness cookies · honey, almond, and basil cheesecake · pistachio and raspberry brownies · instant raw salted caramel chocolate mousse

# Saffron apricots

The quickest, most exotic-tasting dessert I know, made mainly of things that sit happily in your pantry.

I usually use the deep, dark, unsulfured apricots, as I find them more delicious and easier to digest. The cooking time for these will depend on how soft your apricots are—some are only semidried and will cook quicker than the harder, fully dried ones, so adjust your cooking time accordingly.

I use orange blossom water here to add a heady fragrant taste, which I love. If you can't find it, it will work without.

I serve these with a spoonful of coconut yogurt or good thick Greek stuff, and they are equally good on top of some vanilla ice cream, perhaps a dairy-free one.

SERVES 2

3½ ounces/100 g dried apricots
a good pinch of saffron strands
juice of 2 oranges
1 tablespoon orange blossom water
a couple of teaspoons runny honey
yogurt (optional)
chopped pistachios or almonds
(optional)

Put the apricots into a small pan with the saffron and orange juice and bring to a simmer. Simmer for 5 to 10 minutes, until the apricots have softened. Scoop the apricots out and put the orange juice and saffron back on the heat to reduce a little. This will take a couple of minutes.

Allow to cool before spooning the apricots and syrup into bowls. Daintily drizzle over the orange blossom water and squeeze over a little honey. Top with yogurt and some chopped pistachios or almonds, if you like.

# Raw cookie dough bars

I make batches of these in rotation with my raw brownies from *A Modern Way to Eat*. They sit in a tin in the fridge for times when only a hit of something sweet will do. They are one of those magical things that are as delicious as they are good for you.

Raw cookie dough from the bowl was one of my favorite childhood sneaked treats, along with that Ben & Jerry's ice cream that has thick chunks of cookie dough peppered through it. This is my new cookie dough, in a bar: just as delicious.

.......................................................................................................................................................

Line an approximately 8-inch/20-cm-square brownie pan with parchment paper.

First put the Brazil nuts into a food processor and process until they are a fine flour—don't overprocess or they will become nut butter. Add the honey, coconut sugar, coconut oil, and vanilla and pulse gently until the mixture just comes together in a ball. Coarsely chop the chocolate into small pieces.

Turn out the dough onto a chopping board and scatter over the chopped chocolate, then use your hands to gently but quickly knead in the chocolate and distribute it through the dough.

Press the mixture into the lined baking sheet and pop into the fridge for a few minutes. The longer you leave them, the firmer they will be before cutting—10 minutes will do, but 30 to 40 minutes is ideal. Cut into 16 pieces and store in the fridge.

MAKES 16 BARS

7 ounces/200 g skinned Brazil nuts

4 tablespoons runny honey

2 tablespoons coconut sugar

3 tablespoons coconut oil

seeds from 1 vanilla pod,
or 1 teaspoon good vanilla extract

3½ ounces/100 g dark chocolate
(70 percent)

# Coconut and goji fudge bites

I spent three school holidays working at my local farm shop. All the other people my age were on the registers or at the pick-your-own huts weighing up baskets of just-picked strawberries and raspberries. But I got the best job by a mile: I was in charge of sweets and fudge.

On my first day, I was led into a room with a bin full of sweets, presented with a huge fudge kettle and given the fudge recipe, and told I had free rein to experiment and make any flavor I wanted. It was, to this day, one of the best jobs I can imagine. My experiments were endless: raspberry and cardamom fudge in summer, blackberry and bay fudge in autumn, and mulled wine brown sugar fudge at Christmas.

This is my nod to those days of carefree fudge-making, though after months of making the stuff and unwrapping thousands of packages of butter, I favor a fudge made from more virtuous ingredients. This is a brilliant gift for anyone, but especially for someone who's feeling under the weather, as these little fudge bites are packed with goodness.

Goji berries have a lovely flavor, sweet and tangy, and a striking color. On top of that, they are one of the kings of the food world—they are a complete protein, so they're great if you eat a completely vegetarian diet, and they're one of the highest-antioxidant foods in the world.

MAKES 24 BITES

7 ounces/200 g cashews

3½ ounces/100 g desiccated coconut

sea salt

zest and juice of 1 small unwaxed lemon

¼ teaspoon ground cardamom

seeds from 1 vanilla pod, or 1 tablespoon good vanilla extract

3 tablespoons thick honey

4 tablespoons coconut milk or water

1¾ ounces/50 g goji berries

Fill and boil a kettle of water and get all your ingredients and equipment together. Weigh out all your ingredients. You'll need a food processor, a mixing bowl, and a small, deep container for the fudge. Line your container with parchment paper.

In a food processor, blend the cashews, coconut, a good pinch of salt, lemon zest, and cardamom until you have a fine powder. It's important that it's a powder, as otherwise the fudge will be grainy. If you have a less powerful food processor, this may take a few minutes.

Once you have a fine powder, add the vanilla, honey, and lemon juice and pulse until it comes together into a ball. Add the coconut milk and pulse again.

Pour some hot water over the goji berries and leave for 30 seconds to soften a bit, then drain really well and pat dry with paper towels.

Scoop the fudge mixture into your lined container and push it down with the back of a spoon to even it out to a ½-inch/1.5-cm-thick layer. Scatter over the goji berries, put into the fridge to firm up for about 20 minutes, then cut into little squares.

# Rhubarb, apple, and maple pan crumble

I love desserts, but I'm not much of a planner, so it's rare, unless I have people over, that I think to make them in advance—most of the time they are a quick reaction to a craving for something sweet after dinner. So, while I love a crumble, I really only make them on a weekend after a big family meal. This is a crumble you can make any night of the week, and it's filled with good nutrient-packed stuff and natural coconut sugar, so you can eat it with a smile.

Any orchard fruit or stone fruit would work well here. I like plums and pears in autumn and apricots and apples in summer. Dried fruits like prunes work well too. And, if you like, a swig of sloe gin or Armagnac would do nicely. If you can't get coconut sugar, a soft light brown sugar will work, but it won't be as virtuous.

**SERVES 2 GENEROUSLY**

FOR THE FRUIT
7 ounces/200 g apples (about 2)
7 ounces/200 g rhubarb
2 tablespoons coconut sugar
juice of ½ an orange

FOR THE CRUMBLE TOPPING
a small handful of skin-on almonds
(about 1½ ounces/45 g)
5 tablespoons rolled oats
1 tablespoon coconut sugar
coconut oil or butter
1 tablespoon maple syrup

yogurt (I use coconut), to serve

Get all your ingredients together and put two frying pans over medium heat.

Peel the apples and chop into thin slices, then trim the rhubarb and chop it into slices about the same size. Put both fruits into one of the pans with the sugar and the orange juice and cook for 5 minutes, until soft but still holding their shape.

Coarsely chop the almonds. Put the oats and almonds into another pan and toast over low heat for a few minutes. Add the sugar and stir until the sugar starts to melt a little, then quickly take off the heat and add the coconut oil or butter and the maple syrup.

Spoon the fruit into bowls and top with a sprinkling of the crumble. Serve with yogurt.

# Chocolate and Earl Grey pudding pots

These are ten-minute chocolate puddings that are unreasonably delicious considering how little effort goes into making them. They are rich, creamy, and custardy, with a subtle back-note of Earl Grey.

They use tofu as a base. If you think that's weird, you won't be alone, but it makes a creamy, incredibly delicious pudding without having to pour in half a container of cream.

Instead of Earl Grey you could add all sorts of other flavorings here, such as the zest and juice of an orange or a lime and a shot of rum, or even brewed and strained green tea.

Be sure to buy good-quality organic silken tofu for this; it usually comes in a small sealed Tetra Pak. The firm stuff won't work. The quality of tofu you buy is important, as soy crops are some of the most modified and messed around with on the planet; if you can, buy organic.

This recipe can easily be doubled or tripled if you are feeding a crowd. And these pots work well with raspberries, strawberries, clementines, and blood oranges if you'd like some fruit on the side.

......................................................................................................................

SERVES 4

1 Earl Grey tea bag

10 ounces/300 g silken tofu

3½ ounces/100 g dark chocolate (minimum 70 percent)

¼ cup/70 ml maple syrup

1 teaspoon vanilla paste, or the seeds from 1 vanilla pod

1¾ ounces/50 g dark chocolate for grating (optional)

flaked sea salt (optional)

Fill and boil a kettle of water and get all your ingredients together. Pour ½ cup/100 ml of boiling water over the tea bag and leave to steep.

Put the tofu inside a clean kitchen towel or cloth and wring out as much moisture as you can.

Put a pan over low heat and add about ¾ inch/2 cm of boiling water from the kettle. Place a heatproof bowl over the pan, add the chocolate and maple syrup, and leave to melt.

CONTINUED

Put the drained tofu into a food processor. Remove the tea bag from the tea and discard, then add the tea to the processor with the vanilla. Blend until smooth, then add the melted chocolate mixture and blend again until really smooth and silky.

Spoon the mixture into four ramekins and place in the fridge to firm up a little. When you are ready to serve, top with a grating of chocolate and a pinch of flaked sea salt, if you like.

# Banana, date, and candied pecan ice cream

A fast and healthy ice cream. Granted, this does require you to have some frozen bananas in your freezer, but I always freeze any overripe ones for ice creams and smoothies. Be sure to peel and coarsely chop your bananas before you freeze them.

The pecan topping elevates this quick ice cream to another level of deliciousness, adding crunch, texture, and some natural sweetness from the pecans and maple. It makes a super quick and simple topping for store-bought ice cream too.

Get all your ingredients together and put four bowls or glasses into the freezer to cool. Line a heatproof plate or bowl with a piece of parchment paper.

First, make your candied pecans. Heat a frying pan over medium heat, then chop the pecans coarsely and add to the pan to toast a little. Once the nuts have started to brown and are smelling great, add the maple syrup and continue to cook for a further minute. Transfer to your lined heatproof plate or bowl, taking care not to touch the pecans, as the sugar will be really hot.

Put the frozen bananas into the bowl of a food processor with all the other ice cream ingredients. Process on high for 3 to 5 minutes, depending on how powerful your blender is, until you have a smooth ice cream.

If you are not eating your ice cream right away, you can put it into the cold glasses and put them back into the freezer for up to half an hour—but not too much longer, otherwise it will set hard and won't be soft and scoopable.

SERVES 4

FOR THE PECANS

3½ ounces/100 g pecans

2 tablespoons maple syrup

FOR THE ICE CREAM

3 frozen bananas (see headnote)

5 medjool dates, pitted

1 teaspoon vanilla paste, or the seeds from ½ a vanilla pod

a good pinch of ground cinnamon

3½ ounces/100 g coconut cream, or the cream from the top of a can of coconut milk

# Coconut, rhubarb, and lime panna cotta

My all-time friend and kitchen babe Emily made these especially for me, as they have all my favorite things packed into a perky little pudding. A good vegetarian panna cotta is a hard thing to come by, but Emily has crushed the formula here: just-the-right-side-of-sweet rhubarb hidden below barely set coconut, lime, and vanilla custard. All vegan: dairy-, refined sugar–, and, most importantly, gelatin-free. You'll want to thank Em yourself, as this dessert will make your life better.

Agar agar is a clever natural setting agent made from seaweed that you can use just like gelatin. Make sure it's fully dissolved before you pour it into the pudding or you may get a grainy texture.

...............................................................................................................................

Get all your ingredients and equipment together.

Put the coconut milk, coconut water, lime zest, maple syrup, vanilla bean paste, and agar agar into a small saucepan and set aside.

Finely slice the rhubarb and put it into a medium frying pan with a dollop of coconut oil. Place over medium heat, add the coconut sugar, and cook until the rhubarb starts to break down a little. Add the juice of the lime and continue to cook for a further 6 to 8 minutes, or until you are left with a thick, almost jam-like consistency. Remove from the heat and leave to cool.

Place the pan of coconut mixture over medium heat and bring to a boil, without stirring. Once it's boiling, turn down the heat and simmer for 6 minutes, or until the agar agar has dissolved completely.

Place 2 tablespoons of rhubarb in the bottom of four ring molds, coffee cups, or small ceramic bowls. Pour the coconut mixture into a jug, and slowly, so that you don't disturb the layer of rhubarb, pour it into your molds. Chill in the fridge for at least 3 hours. When you're ready to serve, dip the bottom of each mold in boiling water and turn out onto plates.

SERVES 4

1 (14-ounce/400-g) can of coconut milk
⅞ cup/200 ml coconut water
zest and juice of 1 unwaxed lime
scant ½ cup/100 ml maple syrup
1 teaspoon vanilla bean paste
1 heaping tablespoon agar agar
17 ounces/500 g bright pink rhubarb
coconut oil
¾ cup/120 g coconut sugar

# Salted almond butter chocolate bars

A friend said these were the nicest chocolate bars he had ever tasted and that if they were on sale in the shops, he would buy one every day. I think I would too. These little bars are a triumph.

They are packed with goodness and have just a little sweetness from the honey and the dark chocolate. If you want to keep things really pure here, you could use raw honey and raw chocolate for maximum nourishment.

These bars keep really well for a few weeks stacked in a container in the fridge and they freeze brilliantly, so a sweet hit that's full of goodness is never too far away. I make a batch of these every couple of weeks, though they have become a favorite in my house so rarely last more than a few days.

.....................................................................................

Fill and boil a kettle of water and get all your ingredients and equipment together. Line a small square baking pan with baking parchment.

Put the almonds into the bowl of a food processor and process for 5 minutes, until the nuts are beginning to turn into a soft butter. Add the honey or agave syrup, the coconut oil, vanilla, and a good pinch of salt and process to combine. Add the desiccated coconut and process again until you have a scruffy dough-like mixture.

Tip the dough into the lined baking pan and use clean wet hands to even it out into a square about ¾ inch/2 cm thick.

Put the baking pan into the freezer for a couple of minutes. Break the chocolate into a bowl that will comfortably sit on top of one of your pans. Put the pan on the heat, add a couple of centimeters of boiling water and bring to a gentle simmer. Place the bowl on top of the

MAKES 24 BARS

7 ounces/200 g almonds

3 tablespoons runny honey
or agave syrup

2 tablespoons melted coconut oil

seeds from 1 vanilla pod,
or 1 teaspoon good vanilla extract

sea salt

5 ounces/150 g unsweetened
desiccated coconut

7 ounces/200 g dark chocolate
(70 percent)

Flaked sea salt

CONTINUED

pan and let the chocolate melt, making sure the bowl doesn't touch the simmering water.

Take the almond mixture out of the freezer and cut it into 24 bars. I do this by making six vertical slices and four horizontal ones. Pop them back into the freezer to chill.

Once the chocolate has melted, take it off the heat and allow it to cool and thicken, stirring occasionally. Cooling the chocolate a little is important, so that the bars will be thickly coated.

Line a baking sheet with parchment. Take the frozen bars out of the fridge and dip them into the chocolate, using two forks to turn them, then lay them on the parchment. Add a sprinkle of sea salt. Once you have coated all the bars, put them into the fridge to set, about 2 hours.

# Honey and orange ricotta
# and baked figs

This is one of my favorite things to make for a quick, amazing dessert when I have friends over. It is speedy enough for a weeknight too.

Baking ricotta is the easiest thing in the world, but people always seem amazed by it. Get good sheep's milk ricotta if you can.

This is a good way to use up figs that are a little green or out of season, as roasting sweetens them up. This also works well with plums, apricots, or halved strawberries.

I serve this with some little toasts for scooping up the ricotta.

.........................................................................................................................

Preheat your oven to 400°F/200°C (convection 375°F/180°C) and get all your ingredients together. Line a rimmed baking sheet with a sheet of parchment paper.

Turn the ricotta out onto the parchment-lined sheet and drizzle over the honey. Grate over the orange zest and scrape over the vanilla seeds.

SERVES 4 TO 6

9 ounces/250 g ricotta cheese
1 tablespoon runny honey
1 unwaxed orange
seeds from 1 vanilla pod
6 fresh figs
1¾ ounces/50 g almonds

Halve the figs and scatter around the ricotta, then squeeze over the juice of half the orange, drizzle over a little more honey, and put into the oven to bake for 20 minutes.

Coarsely chop the almonds and scatter over everything for the last 5 minutes.

Serve straight from the oven in the middle of the table. Any leftovers can be scooped onto warm toast the next day.

# Cranachan

A super simple and quick dessert that always reminds me of a brilliant Scottish chef I worked with called Pete. I am sure Pete would like me to douse this in whisky, and if that's your thing, do it—I'm sure it would be wonderful.

This is my lighter take on cranachan, a Scottish quartet of raspberries, oats, brown sugar or honey, and cream. I use yogurt (often coconut milk yogurt) instead of cream, and lovely Scottish honey. Toasting the oats gives a satisfying biscuity flavor. This could even be eaten for breakfast.

**SERVES 2 TO 4,
DEPENDING ON APPETITE**

3½ ounces/100 g fresh
or frozen raspberries

1¾ ounces/50 g walnuts

2 tablespoons rolled oats

a pinch of ground cinnamon

a good grating of fresh nutmeg

2 tablespoons runny honey

8 tablespoons Greek yogurt
or coconut yogurt

1 tablespoon bee pollen (optional)

Get all your ingredients together and put a frying pan over medium heat. If using frozen raspberries, get them out now so they soften slightly. Coarsely chop the walnuts, put them into the frying pan along with the oats, and toast for a couple of minutes, until the oats are starting to turn golden. Take off the heat and add the cinnamon, nutmeg, and 1 tablespoon of the honey.

Crush half the raspberries with a fork and fold them into the yogurt, then stir in a bit more honey. Add the remaining whole raspberries, then fold in the toasted oatmeal and spoon into little glasses or bowls. If you like, you can sprinkle a little bee pollen over the top of each. Dainty and amazingly good for you.

# quick fruit desserts

I have a sweet tooth and I like to finish my meal with something delicious and a little sweet but goodness-packed too. Sometimes it's a snap of dark chocolate, but other times it's a quick fruit dessert. Here are some ideas for fruit desserts that are all ready in less than 10 minutes.

## QUICK FRUIT AND YOGURT

Use your favorite yogurt
(mine's coconut)

STRAWBERRIES, PISTACHIOS,
ORANGE ZEST

•

PAPAYA, LIME, DESICCATED COCONUT

•

RASPBERRIES, ROSE WATER,
TOASTED HAZELNUTS

•

DATES, PISTACHIOS, ORANGE,
ORANGE BLOSSOM WATER

•

APRICOTS, PEACHES, LEMON,
VANILLA, TOASTED ALMONDS

## QUICK FRUIT SALADS

5 favorite combinations

WATERMELON, CHERRIES,
GRAPES, RASPBERRIES

•

PERSIMMON, MANGO, LIME,
BLOOD ORANGE

•

APPLES, PEARS, PLUMS,
BLACKBERRIES

•

STRAWBERRIES, LEMON,
VANILLA, PEACHES

•

MANGO, LIME, MINT,
PAPAYA, MELON

## QUICK WARM FRUIT

Warm your fruit under the broiler
or quickly in a pan

PRUNES, ARMAGNAC, VANILLA
(WARMED IN A PAN)

•

PAPAYA, LIME ZEST (UNDER A BROILER)

•

STRAWBERRIES, RHUBARB, MAPLE
SYRUP (WARMED IN A PAN)

•

APRICOTS, HONEY, VANILLA
(UNDER A BROILER)

•

PLUMS, CINNAMON, HONEY
(UNDER A BROILER)

## QUICK FRUIT ICE CREAM

Make instant ice cream by puréeing
frozen fruit—try these for starters

FROZEN BANANA, HONEY

•

FROZEN BERRIES, VANILLA

•

FROZEN RASPBERRIES, LEMON

•

FROZEN PINEAPPLE, LIME

•

FROZEN WATERMELON = SORBET

## QUICK
## CHOCOLATE SAUCE

to accompany the ice creams

3½ OUNCES/100 G
MELTED UNSWEETENED
CHOCOLATE

+

2 TABLESPOONS
MAPLE SYRUP

# Dark chocolate goodness cookies

These are chewy, deeply chocolatey cookies. The kind that are so pleasingly dense, gooey, and satisfying that even the greediest cookie eater can only manage a couple.

They aren't run-of-the-mill cookies, though. They're made from one of my favorite ingredients, though not one you might associate with baking—black beans. The fudgy, slightly sweet character of black beans works so well in baking, and of the numerous people I have asked to guess what is in these, so far no one has picked them out.

I have kept the double chocolate pretty pure here, but you could easily add some lemon or orange zest, raisins, or sour cherries. For a more traditional chocolate chip cookie, you can swap the black beans for cannellini beans.

Oh, and did I mention these are naturally free of gluten, dairy, and refined sugar? Almost virtuous deliciousness.

MAKES ABOUT 10 COOKIES

2 tablespoons chia seeds,
or 2 free-range or organic eggs

½ cup/125 ml maple syrup

1 teaspoon vanilla extract

1 (14-ounce/400-g) can of
black beans

2 tablespoons coconut oil

6 tablespoons/40 g cocoa powder

a good pinch of flaky sea salt,
plus more for sprinkling

2½ ounces/75 g dark chocolate
(70 percent)

1¾ ounces/50 g medjool dates

Preheat your oven to 400°F/210°C (convection 375°F/190°C). Get all your ingredients together and line a baking sheet with parchment paper.

If you are using chia seeds, mix them with 4 tablespoons of cold water. Mix the chia mixture or the eggs with the maple syrup and vanilla in a bowl and set aside.

Drain your beans, rinse well under cold water, then put them into a food processor with the coconut oil, cocoa, and salt and blend until you have a smooth dough.

Add the maple syrup mixture and pulse until you have a wet dough. The batter will be quite liquid but will still hold together.

Scoop the whole lot out into a bowl. Chop the chocolate and the dates and stir into the dough.

Spoon a generous tablespoon of the batter onto the lined baking sheet and use the back of the spoon to flatten the top to a cookie shape, as they will not spread very much when baked. Sprinkle the tops with a little flaky salt and bake for 12 to 15 minutes, until the edges are browning.

# Honey, almond, and basil cheesecake

This is my super-quick version of the cheesecake that has been raved about from a London restaurant called Honey and Co. Theirs is much posher and more complicated. Mine takes 10 minutes. We are meeting in the middle.

I use shredded wheat here, which you might think sounds rather weird, but it is my attempt at quickly mimicking the brilliant shards of kadaif pastry that sit below the strained feta at Honey and Co. I think it works pretty well.

Shredded wheat is one of the last true cereals, and when I was growing up, it was what my dad ate for breakfast every morning. Unlike most cereals, it has no additives, and you can buy organic versions in health food shops too. I often use soft feta cheese here, which I can buy easily in my local shop, but ricotta will work just as well if soft feta is not easy for you to come by.

Get all your ingredients together.

Put a pan over medium heat and, once it's hot, add the almonds and cook for a minute or two until they smell toasty. Put into a bowl for later.

Put the pan back on the heat, add 3 tablespoons of honey, and crumble in the shredded wheat. Heat for a couple of minutes, tossing all the time to coat the shredded wheat with the honey. Take off the heat.

Whip the ricotta or feta in a bowl with the vanilla, the final tablespoon of honey, and the zest of half the lemon, using a handheld electric mixer (or a balloon whisk and some determination), until smooth, whipped, and cloudy. If you are using it, stir in the orange blossom water. Coarsely chop the cooled almonds.

Divide the honey-glazed shreds among plates and top with a generous spoonful of the ricotta. Scatter over the berries and almonds and some torn mint or basil, and drizzle with a little more honey, if you like.

SERVES 4

a handful of skinned almonds

4 tablespoons runny honey, plus more for drizzling

2 large biscuits shredded wheat

9 ounces/250 g good ricotta or soft Greek feta cheese

1 tablespoon vanilla paste

1 unwaxed lemon

a dash of orange blossom water (optional)

a couple of handfuls of seasonal berries

a few sprigs of mint or basil

# Pistachio and raspberry brownies

These brownies are for my mom and dad. They love life and are the two best people I know. They are also, in the nicest possible way, chalk and cheese, so finding things they both love can be hard, and this is where these pretty perfect brownies come in. My dad loves chocolate; my mom loves raspberries and pistachios. Here all the things they love come together in a ridiculously delicious harmony.

These dense, gooey, and chocolatey brownies are made with ground almonds and coconut sugar, so they are a little lighter and more nutrient-packed than your average brownie. I almost always make these with chia seeds in place of the eggs, which makes them vegan too. If you use chia seeds, you'll need to add a little baking powder to make sure the brownies rise.

Frozen raspberries work really well here, and in the summer I sometimes make these with pitted halved cherries too. If coconut sugar is a bridge too far, then soft brown sugar will work too.

MAKES 12 BROWNIES

3 organic or free-range eggs, beaten, or 3 tablespoons chia seeds

7 ounces/200 g dark chocolate (70 percent)

5 ounces/150 g coconut oil or unsalted butter

1½ cups/250 g coconut sugar

1 teaspoon natural vanilla extract, or the seeds from 1 vanilla pod

5 ounces/150 g ground almonds

1 heaping teaspoon baking powder (if you are using chia seeds, not eggs)

4 ounces/125 g raspberries (frozen or fresh)

1¾ ounces/50 g pistachios

Preheat the oven to 350°F/180°C (convection 325°F/160°C) and get all your ingredients and equipment together. Grease a small brownie pan with coconut oil or butter and line it with parchment paper (mine is 8 by 8 inches/20 by 20 cm but anything around that size will do).

If you are using chia seeds rather than eggs, put the seeds into a little bowl and add 9 tablespoons of cold water. Leave to form a gel-like paste.

Place a heatproof bowl over a pan of gently simmering water, making sure the bowl doesn't touch the water. Put 5 ounces/150 g of the chocolate into the bowl with the coconut oil or butter and let them melt, stirring from time to time. Take the bowl off the heat and stir in the sugar, followed by the

⋮· CONTINUED

beaten eggs, one by one, or the chia seed mixture, and finally the vanilla, ground almonds, and the baking powder, if using, plus half the raspberries (if they are frozen, don't defrost them first) and half the pistachios. Coarsely chop the remaining 1¾ ounces/50 g of chocolate and fold through the mixture too.

Pour the brownie mixture into the lined pan and scatter over the rest of the raspberries and the pistachios. Bake for 25 to 30 minutes, until just cooked but still a little soft in the middle.

Leave to cool for at least 20 minutes before cutting. These will keep for 3 to 4 days, but I challenge you to make them last that long!

# Instant raw salted caramel chocolate mousse

I am not one of those healthy eaters who likes things to taste wholesome, so don't be put off when you read the virtuous ingredient list for this dessert. I want chocolate to be rich, indulgent, and craveworthy.

It's a recipe I feel a bit embarrassed writing down, as it is so, so simple, but often those are the best.

A powerful blender works best here, but failing that, a handheld blender and a bit of elbow grease will do just fine. For best results, make sure your banana is frozen and your avocado and lemon are fridge-cold. And be sure not to use a really large banana, or the flavor of banana will be overpowering.

I have left the serving size a little ambiguous—this is rich, so some might like a dainty cupful, while real chocolate lovers might like a bit more. It's easily doubled or even tripled for parties and keeps well in the fridge for a few hours.

**SERVES 2 TO 4**

**FOR THE MOUSSE**

1 ripe avocado

1 small frozen banana

juice of ½ lemon or lime

3 tablespoons cocoa powder (I use the raw stuff)

2 tablespoons maple syrup

**FOR THE SALTED CARAMEL SAUCE**

6 medjool dates

2 tablespoons maple syrup

sea salt

Get all your ingredients together. Put all the mousse ingredients into a blender with a tablespoon of cold water and purée on high until everything is whipped to a smooth mousse, stopping to scrape down the sides a couple of times—this may take a couple of minutes in a less powerful blender. Scoop it out into cups and give the blender a quick rinse.

Put the pitted dates into the blender (if your blender is large, a handheld blender might work better here) with the maple syrup, a tablespoon of cold water, and a good pinch of sea salt. Blend until you have a thick, smooth caramel sauce. Drizzle the sauce on top of the mousse and top with some extra salt crystals.

# Acknowledgments

This book, in keeping with its theme, came together in quite a short time. This was made more joyful and much less stressful by the amazing group of people I feel lucky enough to call my family and friends.

Firstly to John "Ideas Man" Dale, your belief in me is unwavering, and your constant, gentle support is all I could ever wish for. You know how much of this belongs to you. I can't wait to marry you on the island and for our next adventure.

To Mom and Dad, the kindness, love, and support you continue to send my way leaves me lost for words. The freedom and belief you've afforded and instilled in me have meant I have been free to follow my own path, and to me that is the greatest gift you could have given. You are truly my two favorite people.

To Laura, my sister, I look to you for everything, and always have; thank you for striving to be the best you can be in every way, and in doing so, bringing me along with you. Thank you too for so generously sharing all your food discoveries and ideas, many of which fill the pages of this book.

To Owen, my brother, the youngest but also somehow the wisest in our family; you are a true individual, a kind soul, a trailblazer. You are led by what's right, and if more people in the world were like you, we'd be a lot better off. I am really proud of you.

To Emily, your help making this book what it is went above and beyond—helping me out when inspiration was lacking and keeping me going when the task seemed insurmountable. You are a truly incredible, generous, and brilliantly creative soul. This book would not have been written without you. Thank you.

To Louise Haines, I am humbled by your belief in me and my cooking. Thank you for caring so much about every detail of this book. Working with you in your brilliant organic way is a joy, and I feel very lucky to be published by you and 4th Estate.

To Georgia Mason, the most wonderful editor, in the shortest of timescales you have held this book together as if it were your own, which in part it undoubtedly is. I am so grateful for every single thing you have done to make me as proud of this book as I am.

Thank you, too, to Annie Lee for your close eye, and to Morwenna Loughman for all your help.

To Matt Russell, you have made this book come alive. Again under tight timelines you put everything into this, at the same time as leaving your ego at the door; it's a rare and generous skill. I think your photographs are just brilliant. Thank you. To Ollie, Matt's assistant, thank you for your island charm; the shoots were so much better for your presence.

To Sandra, who designed this book with such grace, thank you; you have worked stupidly hard to make this the book it is. I am in awe of your dedication and creativity. I can't tell you how much it means to know you care as much as I do. Thank you.

To Michelle Kane, thank you in advance for the amazing things I know you have up your sleeve. Thanks, too, to all the papers, magazines, and blogs that allowed me to grace their pages, especially Allan Jenkins and the team at OFM.

To Jess, thank you for everything, for taking it all so brilliantly in your stride; you are a rare combination of shining creativity and amazing pragmatism. I feel very lucky to have you around.

To Alex Gray, thanks for all your hard work in the kitchen, your amazing lunches; you are a true gentleman.

To amazing friends who helped test the recipes in this book, you are incredible; thank you. Your notes, comments, and feedback give me such confidence in the recipes in this book and I am so grateful for every single meal you cooked. Krys Gaffney, Ceri Tallett, James Bannochie and Emma Ballinger, James Gold, Angelique Mercier, Jon and Laura Plane, Anna and Ellen Fermie, Olenka Lawrenson, Emily Taylor, Bryony Walker, Sian Dale, Sian Tallett, Danny McCubbin, Anja Forrest Dunk, Mimi Beaven, Mersedeh Prewer, Lizzie Winn, Priya Thakar, Eileen Power, Ella Power, Alice Power, Philippa Spence, Christina Mackenzie, Alex Grimes, Carys Williams, Nick and Anna Probert, Kris Hallenga, Luke Shaller.

Some amazing friends have helped this book on its way. To Ceri Tallett, the best in the business, thank you for your eye, your words, and your generosity, which is actually endless. Now it's your turn. I want a Tallett on my bookshelf. To Liz, you have skills I wish I had, thanks for sharing them with me and keeping me on track. You are gold. To Crystal, my cousin, an all-in-one Anna Jones PR machine. You are unstoppable, thanks for all your help.

To Brickett Davda, The Conran Shop, David Mellor, and Labour and Wait, thank you all for trusting me with your insanely beautiful things. I pretended they were mine for a few weeks; it was hard to give them back. You are all incredibly generous.

To all my friends who for the last six months haven't heard a peep out of me; this book is the reason why. I love you all and look forward to a summer filled with your faces.

And lastly but most importantly, every single person who bought a copy of *A Modern Way to Eat*; to each person who cooked a recipe, to everyone who looked at my blog. You all inspire me every day. I love reading your e-mails and seeing the pictures of things you have made. It still blows me away every time. I am so thankful that we are all on this journey together. You are all amazing.

## About the Author

Anna Jones is a cook, food writer, and stylist. She worked for many years as part of Jamie Oliver's food team—styling, writing, and working behind the scenes on books, TV shows, and food campaigns—and went on to work with some of the UK's biggest food brands and best-known chefs. She is the author of *A Modern Way to Eat*, widely acclaimed as a book of the year. *A Modern Way to Cook* is her second book. She lives, writes, and cooks in Hackney, East London.

# Index

**The following recipes are vegan or gluten-free, or require only simple tweaking to adapt them.**

All rights reserved.
Published in the United States by Ten Speed Press,
an imprint of the Crown Publishing Group, a division
of Penguin Random House LLC, New York.
www.crownpublishing.com
www.tenspeed.com

Ten Speed Press and the Ten Speed Press colophon are
registered trademarks of Penguin Random House LLC.

All photographs by Matt Russell except images on pages
22, 54, 102, 148,224, 278, and 304.

Originally published in slightly different form in hardcover
in Great Britain by Fourth Estate, an imprint
of HarperCollinsPublishers, London, in 2015.

Library of Congress Cataloging-in-Publication Data
is on file with the publisher.

Hardcover ISBN: 978-0-399-57842-7
eBook ISBN: 978-0-399-57843-4

Printed in China

10 9 8 7 6 5 4 3 2

First United States Edition, 2016